JAMES JOYCE

UNPLUGGED

Introduction

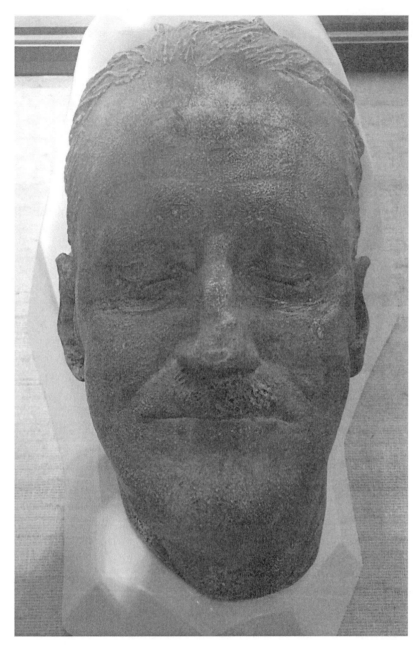

James Joyce death mask.

JAMES JOYCE

UNPLUGGED

ANTHONY J. JORDAN

ACKNOWLEDGEMENTS

I wish to thank the following for assistance in the project:
Brid O'Sullivan of the National Library, Gerard Whelan RDS Library,
Elizabeth Turley Pembroke Library, Luke Gibbons of NUIM, Ringsend Library,
National Archives, Maire Kennedy Gilbert Library, Ambassador Dan Mulhall,
Luke Gibbons, Kay Gleeson, Declan McIlraith, Seamus Cannon, James
Holihan, Rodney Devitt, Elizabeth Keane, Judith Jordan.

Thanks to Sean Kehoe, Patrick Hugh Lynch & Joyce Tower Museum for
photographs. Thanks to Patrick O'Keeffe for proof-reading text.

Cover design by Sean Kehoe

Printed by Sprint-Print, Rathcoole, Co. Dublin.

Published by Westport Books Dublin 4.

INTRODUCTION

While researching my biography of Arthur Griffith[1] I read copies of his newspaper *The United Irishman* on microfilm. In one copy dated 2 November 1901, I noticed the name of James Joyce in the text. I gradually uncovered the unlikely relationship between the two men, which reached its culmination with the publication of *Ulysses* in 1922 and Griffith's accession to the Presidency of Dail Eireann. Griffith is the only contemporary politician of the period who features throughout the novel as newspaper editor and founder of Sinn Fein. I am regularly surprised to meet people who have 'read' *Ulysses* and do not recollect this aspect of the novel!

Andras Ungar argues that Joyce's *Ulysses* is the Irish national epic, exploring the parallel between the program of Arthur Griffith and Sinn Fein and the meetings of Stephen Daedalus and Leopold Bloom, with their dreams of self-expression and continuity[2]. Joyce told his brother Stanislaus that were it not for the Irish language he could probably call himself an Irish nationalist.
Declan Kiberd writes, *Like Yeats, Joyce presented himself as a modern Homer, a type of the epic narrator even in his reluctance to begin*[3].

The James Joyce Tower Museum in Dublin was opened in 1962 by Sylvia Beach. A high proportion of the visitors come from abroad. I recall an Italian lady, in full praise of Joyce, saying so accurately, *'The great thing Joyce did was to create an international community'*. I have one *caveat* with many of the visitors; they only know Joyce from his fiction. Though this was largely autobiographical, as a biographer I feel they are missing out somewhat on engaging with

---

[1] . Jordan Anthony J., *Arthur Griffith with James Joyce and WB Yeats – Liberating Ireland*, Westport Books 2013.
[2] . Ungar Andras, *Joyce's Ulysses As National Epic*, University Florida 2002.
[3] . Kiberd Declan, *Inventing Ireland*, Vintage 1996, p. 355.

Joyce the Dubliner, the Irishman self-exiled in Europe, who retained and perpetuated love of country, becoming an Irish nationalist, insofar as that was possible for his persona.

At a lecture in the National Library in June 2016, Professor Luke Gibbons of Irish Literary and Cultural Studies at Maynooth University lectured on the title of *'Proclaiming Self and Nation: Joyce's Portrait and the Easter Rising'*. He said that Joyce was very keen that *A Portrait of the Artist as a Young Man* be published in 1916. In keeping with Joyce's vision, the Easter Rising is best conceived in modernist terms, as an event before its time. In its approaches to language, narrative and history, the Rising on the streets of Dublin, paralleled many of the innovative approaches to time and space adopted by Joyce in the writing of *Portrait* and *Ulysses*. Joyce saw *Portrait* creating not only the *'conscience'* of the self but of the *'race'*, and in this, his project was akin to the revolutionary gesture of the Proclamation of 1916. Declan Kiberd said that *"Joyce wrote from the viewpoint of a staunch republican"*[4].

One aspect of a Joyce biography which requires elucidation and explanation is his apparent belief that because he was writing first class material, this afforded him the right to ignore the common social and moral rules of a civilised society. WB Yeats adopted a similar modus operandi and explained it that as he was *'a writer of tragic art'*, the social mores that applied to everyone else did not apply to him. To assuage his betrayal of Lady Gregory in 1910, Yeats regarded reason as almost blasphemous, the stopping of the pendulum, the wearing of a mask, but as an artist with irreconcilable attitudes towards life, constrained to avoid general standards thoughts[5].

---

[4] . Kiberd Declan, Irish Times Supplement on Home Rule 25/4/12012.
[5] . Jordan Anthony J. Jordan, *WB Yeats. Vain, Glorious, Lout; A Maker of Modern Ireland*. Westport Books 2003. p. 23.

When Andre Gide commented that Joyce's courage in carrying his literary experiments to the limit, indifferent to success or money, had something saintly about it, Sylvia Beach's partner, Adrienne Monnier, wrote to Joyce; *'What Gide doesn't know is that you are, on the contrary, very concerned about success and you wish others also to go to the limit; you lead by rough stages to some Dublingrad or other place, which they're not interested in...'.*

Roger Norburn has identified sums of monies received by Joyce from a variety of Patrons over the years and calculated that they totalled £1.8 million in 2004 sterling value[6].

On his death, Nora Joyce hoped that her husband's body would one day return to his homeland.

To commemorate the centenary of the publication of *Portrait of the Artist as a Young Man* on 29 December 2016, the Irish novelist Rob Doyle wrote, *"It's likely that if I went back to Portrait now I'd have a better, if still frosty, appreciation of its stylistic inventions... I never cared much for Dubliners either. It was only when I got on to Ulysses that I realised what a stupendously renegade, subversive, ambitious, perverse and perverted talent Joyce was"*[7].

---

[6]. Norburn Roger, *A James Joyce Chronology*, Palgrave MacMillan 2004. p. 199. The exact amount was £1,844,130.
[7]. Irish Times 29/12/2016.

Chapter 1.

Pupil at Clongowes and Belvedere

James Joyce's family came from Cork. His grandfather, James Augustine Joyce had improved the status of the family by marrying into the prosperous family of the O'Connell's at the age of 21 years in 1848. His wife Ellen had been briefly in the Presentation nuns. James Augustine, who was a *bon vivant* succeeded in becoming bankrupt within a few years of marriage but was then successful in securing a steady job as an Inspector of Hackney Coaches. Their only child, James' father, John Stanislaus, was born in 1849. He became the youngest student attending St Colman's College Fermoy, a junior seminary, at the age of ten. He studied music but stayed for less than one year, leaving with his fees unpaid. His father died at the age of thirty nine in 1866 when his son was only fifteen. John Stanislaus then became a university student at the Queen's College in Cork where he was an excellent student in academics, athletics and sailing. He devoted so much time to extra-curricular activities, which included starring in the college theatricals that he failed his second arts examinations and had to repeat the year. He failed his finals too but this does not appear to have affected his sense of importance and daring. Several of his theatrical performances received good notices in the *Cork Examiner*. The early death of James Augustine saw his son, John Stanislaus, inherit substantial properties. When he reached his twenty first birthday his Grandfather O'Connell gave him £1,000. Always looking for excitement he went to London with some friends with the intention of volunteering to join the French army in the Franco-Prussian War. His mother intercepted him and returned him to Cork where he tried to join the local Fenians. This led his mother deciding to move from Cork to Dublin, where they lived in Dalkey. Her cousin Peter Paul McSweeney had just been elected Lord Mayor in Dublin and she felt that he might be able to assist her wayward son. Before he left Cork a dinner was held in his honour by his friends. Dalkey was a popular location for a man who was a keen sailor. He resumed his musical education with singing lessons and performed at the Ancient Concert Rooms on what is now Pearse St.

Joyce Family Crest

John was inveigled by another Cork man, Henry Alleyne, to invest in a distillery in Chapelizod. This went well briefly until Alleyn defrauded the Company, forcing closure and loss of investment. John then dabbled in politics as a Home Ruler but then became secretary to the National Liberal Club in Dublin. At the General Election of 1880 two liberal candidates stood trying to defeat the sitting conservatives in Dublin city. John campaigned vigorously and to his surprise, as he observed the counting of votes at the Exhibition Palace, he witnessed the two Liberals unseat their opponents amid great rejoicing. John was paid £100 each by the victorious Liberals. But when the new Liberal Government took office, John was further rewarded by getting the permanent position of Rates Collector for Dublin at £500 per annum. He was noted in Dublin as a precocious Cork man with the gift of good humour and the ability to talk himself into and out of all sorts of situations.

John was a member of the choir in the Three Patrons Church on Rathgar Road. There he had met a young female chorister named Mary Jane Murray whose family in Longford had done business with his distillery. Though ten years younger than John, Mary Jane was a most resolute lady. She knew that John was a heavy drinker and a ladies' man, but she welcomed his advances. Her father was dead against it and challenged both of them. John's mother was against it feeling that the Murrays were not of the same social status as the Joyce's. John then took the audacious step of going to live a few doors away from the Murrays on Clanbrassil St. Mrs Murray, like her daughter's suitor and eventually her husband, relented and the marriage took place at Rathmines Catholic Church on 5 May 1880. Mrs Joyce though had not approved and did not attend the wedding. She had already returned to live in Cork where she later died un-reconciled with her only son. After their honeymoon in London the couple lived at Northumberland Avenue in Dunlaoire, later moving to 41 Brighton Square West in Rathgar. John collected the rates for Inns Quay, Rotunda and North Dock Ward in Dublin city. As his expenditure outpaced his income John began to mortgage his properties in Cork. Their first child James Augustine was born on 2 February 1882 at their new home, 41 Brighton Square, Rathgar. By the time their tenth child, four boys and six girls, had been born in 1894, all his Cork properties had been dissipated through mortgages.

James Joyce aged six and a half, 'Half-Past Six'.

41 Brighton Square, Birthplace of Joyce, Rathgar.

James Augustine was baptised on 5 February at St Joseph's Church Terenure. Two years later the family moved to 23 Castlewood Avenue in Rathmines before, in May 1887, moving to 1 Martello Tce. in Bray to be near the sea. John joined the local rowing club. Their house became a regular centre on Sundays for his friends from Dublin to call, make merry, sing with May Joyce at the piano with John leading the singing. William O'Connell, an elderly relation from Cork came to live with the Joyces in Bray for several years. Their house was near the water's edge from where they had a view southwards to the Esplanade running to Bray Head. Throwing stones into the sea was a favourite pastime until James was badly bitten by a dog that was following their stones. This was the basis for a lifetime's fear of dogs for James[8]. A regular visitor was a Tralee man named John

[8] . Byrne JF. *Silent Years An Autobiography with Memoirs of James Joyce and Our Ireland*. Farrar, Straus and Young New York 1953. P. 156. JF Byrne became a journalist in America.

Kelly, whom John Joyce supported through his jousts with the law on behalf of the Land League. Another was the children's key governess from Cork, Mrs Hearn-Conway or '*Dante*' as she was called. After abandoning religious life she came into money and married. Her husband ran off with her money but she got some solace from being a devout Catholic and nationalist. Dante had a great influence on James, teaching him the three 'r's' and reciting poetry. When lightning struck she taught him to bless himself and say, "*Jesus of Nazareth, King of the Jews, from a sudden and un-provided for death deliver us. O Lord*". James' sight caused problems from an early age. He always appeared a happy child and was referred to in the family as '*Sunny Jim*' while the brother next to him, stubborn Stanislaus, was called '*Brother John*'. The only thing that scared the life out of James was a thunderstorm from which he would flee in desperation to the cupboard.

One of their neighbours on Martello Terrace were the Vances who were Protestants. Mr. Vance and John became great companions socialising together. Eileen Vance was a little younger than James and both their fathers, who were singing companions, used to say the two children might yet make a great match. Dante warned Sunny Jim against playing with the Protestant girl for fear of going to hell. Eileen and James went to the same preschool in Bray and were childhood friends. While he was in Clongowes, a verse purporting to come from her caused embarrassment to both. It read

Oh, Jimmy Joyce, you are my darlin',
You are my looking-glass night and mornin'.
I'd rather have you without a farthin
Than Johnny jones, with his ass and garden.

James' voice was so good that he joined both his parents performing at the Bray Boat Club aged six. John and his wife both sang in the church choir at Little Bray. Home life was fairly pleasant though the father's grandiosity had to be constantly humoured, especially by his wife. The task of rate collecting did not appear to be very onerous but even at that John was not methodical and ran into difficulties with rent arrears.

John naturally thought his eldest son deserved the very best in life. To this end he decided to send him aged six to the Jesuit boarding school Clongowes Wood, forty miles away in Co. Kildare. John could then afford the £25 fee, 'to include everything' reduced from £45, for his boy. Both parents travelled with the little boy by car and handed him over to the soutane-clad priests. It was an emotional parting for each of them as his mother begged him to avoid coarse boys. His father, in his usual pomposity, impressed on the boy that he came from the same lineage as Daniel O'Connell the Liberator, who had once spoken at the School. It must have been a heart-wrenching experience for James to see his parents drive away and home to Bray, leaving him to his own fate in this strange environment. As so many boys have had to do in the past, James had to make do to survive. Peace and relative safety came each night as the boy snuggled beneath the sheets in his bed. All else was exposure to the vicissitudes of his fellow students and priests in class-rooms, study-hall, refectory, playing-fields, walks and chapel. James was initially home-sick though he received special care by being allowed to sleep in the infirmary rather the dormitory, under the watchful eye of a nurse, Nanny Galvin. James was bullied by having his glasses broken by another boy pushing him into a pond. This was compounded by being victimised by the thuggish Prefect of Studies, Fr. Dolan, who called him a "*lazy little schemer. Lazy little loafer. Broke my glasses! An old schoolboy trick! Out with your hand this moment!* Then he slapped him; *...drew back his maimed and quivering right arm and held out his left hand. The soutane sleeve swished again as the pandybat was lifted and a loud crashing sound and a fierce maddeningly tingling burning pain made his hand shrink together with the palms and fingers. His body shook with a palsy of fright and in shame and rage he felt the scalding cry come from his throat and the scalding tears falling out of his eyes and down his flaming cheeks"* Then according to James himself, to the astonishment of his classmates, he was brave and foolhardy enough to take a complaint to the Rector, Fr. Conmee, who gave his some succour. His classmates were thrilled by what he had done, flung their caps in the air and whistled and cried '*Hurroo!*".

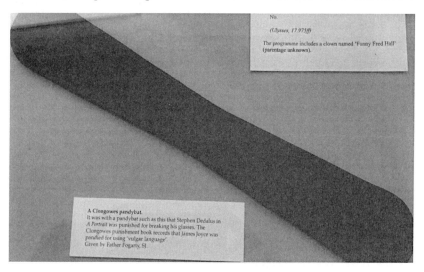

No.

(Ulysses, 17.975ff)

The programme includes a clown named 'Funny Fred Hall' (parentage unknown).

A Clongowes pandybat.
It was with a pandybat such as this that Stephen Dedalus in *A Portrait* was punished for breaking his glasses. The Clongowes punishment book records that James Joyce was pandied for using 'vulgar language'.
Given by Father Fogarty, SJ.

A Pandybat

As often happens in boarding schools, a boy can come into his own and be admired by his fellows for excelling in some activity. Strangely young James did excel at sports of a non-confrontational nature like running, walking, swimming and cricket. He became a

Mass server, always a mark of official approval. But it was as a diligent student especially of religion that he left his mark at Clongowes and specifically on the Rector Fr. Conmee. The world of order and piety and ritual in Catholic services appealed to his senses. For his confirmation he took the name of Aloysius, who feared the temptation of women so greatly that he would not allow his mother to hug him. Essay writing became James' forte. Despite the all-embracing environment of Catholicism the school echoed an English public school curriculum rather than anything inherently Irish.

In June 1891 financial disaster hit the Joyce family. James had to leave Clongowes as the family were forced to move from Bray to Carysfort Ave in Blackrock. Rate collecting was being taken over by Dublin Corporation in 1892 and most staff were being let go. John Joyce's work record was poor. On one occasion he had abandoned his office, travelled to Cork to canvass his tenants to vote for Parnell during the famous Parnell Split. He was not being awarded any pension until his wife appealed the decision. Her extravagant husband with no sense of responsibility towards his large family, and then aged forty one years was awarded £133 per annum.

James enjoyed living at Blackrock. It had a running track and on Sundays his father and Uncle Charles would take him on long walks. He would play with local boys and ride on a milk cart all the way to Carrickmines. Though nobody explained matters to him James realised that his father had got into some sort of trouble. Some of his siblings went to a local convent school but he remained at home studying by himself and tutored by his mother. In a strange way James felt himself transfigured.

In 1892-3 the Joyces were on the move again, this time into the city of Dublin. Their move from Blackrock was abrupt and caused Mrs Joyce to weep. They stayed in lodgings at first but then lived at 14 Fitzgibbon St near Mountjoy Square. It was a bare cheerless house in a large and unknown city. Regular flights from rented accommodation became a feature of their lives. James reacted with an angry embittered silence which did not leave him as he began to explore his surroundings and come to enjoy his loneliness. The main providers of free Catholic education in Dublin were the Christian Brothers. The 'Brothers' were noted for adherence to Catholicism, Nationalism and the Irish language, rigid school rules and academic achievement, despite large classes. Corporal punishment was very common. They had a school at nearby North Richmond St. and very reluctantly John Joyce consigned his boys to that school. Many middle class Irish, people intent on class consciousness, looked down on the 'Brothers' as serving the poor and being composed of people in the main from peasant stock. It is a measure of John Joyce's desperation that he sent his darling protégé boy James, to such a school, where he would not meet and mix with those whose families were rich and therefore important and who would one day themselves inherit such roles in Irish society. From the Jesuits to the Christian Brothers was quite a fall in grace. James himself hardly enjoyed his stay there as he ignored his time with the 'Brothers' entirely in later life, but did put a vicious diatribe about the 'Brothers' in the mouth of his father and mother. In *Portrait of the Artist as a Young Man* he has Mrs Dedalus say, *"I never liked the idea of sending him to the christian brothers myself, said Mrs Dedalus. Christian Brothers be damned! said Mr. Dedalus. Is it with Paddy Stink and Micky Mud? No, let him stick to the Jesuits in God's name since he began with them. They'll be of service to him in after years. Those are the fellows that can get you a position".*

John Joyce was a dapper little man with a military moustache, who sported an eyeglass and cane, and wore spats. When he lost his job he began to enter competitions carried in magazines, especially in *Titbits* and *Answers*. He would study the clues offered with great care. James told Richard Sheehy that his father's current occupation was *"going in for competitions"*[9]. His ebullience and devil-may-care attitude to life was rewarded one day when strolling along Mountjoy Square he met Fr. Conmee, who had been recently transferred from Clongowes to nearby Belvedere College as Prefect of Studies. John, as usual, was quick off the mark in speaking about his precocious son James and how intelligent he was. Though Fr. Conmee had not yet become Provincial of the Jesuits in Ireland, he was influential. John felt that he had to give a version of his misfortune leading to his sons having to attend the Christian Brothers. Fr. Conmee in true Christian fashion, remembering the promise that young James offered, and in no way demeaning the education offered by the *'Brothers'*, agreed that all the Joyce brothers could attend Belvedere, which was a day school, as free boys. James enrolled there on 6 April 1893, followed by his brother Stanislaus. Belvedere posed no problems for the eleven year old boy as he soon began to excel in writing remarkable English compositions. We learn from Stanislaus that a fellow student from Blackrock informed his class mates that the Joyce father had gone bankrupt and had fled Blackrock[10].

When James was home on Christmas holidays from Clongowes one year, a major row developed over Charles Stewart Parnell, whom John Joyce worshipped. At a Christmas family dinner Dante Conway was annoyed by a critical reference to priests made by one of the guests. When further critical references were made about the

[9] . Sheehy Eugene, *May it Please the Court* CJ Fallon.1951. p. 24.

[10] . Joyce Stanislaus, *My Brother's Keeper*. Ed. Richard Ellmann Faber & Faber 1958. P. 71

Church's condemnation of Parnell for his adulterous affair with Mrs O'Shea, Dante again defended the clergy. Despite some of those present trying to move away from the subject, a full blown shouting row occurred between Dante and a gentleman. Dante described Parnell as a *"traitor to his country. The priests were right to abandon him. God and morality and religion come first"*. The gentleman responded, *"No God for Ireland. Away with God. We have had too much God in Ireland. Away with God I say"*, as Dante rushed out of the room and James saw his father weep for Parnell. The Parnell story had become very real for the boys at Clongowes as sons of the man who had forged the Parnell Letters, Richard Piggott were fellow pupils. When Piggott committed suicide in Madrid the boys were warned not to speak of it to his sons. The image of Parnell was to become very important even in myth for James as he compared his own mission in life to that of Parnell's. James wrote a contemporary poem at the age of nine about the October 6 1891 death of the Uncrowned King. A verse of it survives and reads;

Et Tu, Healy
His quaint-perched aerie on the crags of time
Where the rude din of this .... Century
Can trouble him no more

CS Parnell

John Stanislaus Joyce

Tim Healy was one of the politicians who sided with the Church in denouncing Parnell. The literary allusion is to the murder of Caesar by Brutus from Shakespeare's play, *Julius Caesar* and is an example of the precociousness of the young boy. His adoring father had the poem printed and distributed among his many friends.

Another event which was important to James was a trip, lasting about one week, he made to Cork with his father to dispose of the final properties and gain some short financial respite. They rambled round the city visiting the Mardyke, Queen's College, the Presentation convent and the seaside at Crosshaven, as James gained an insight about how vital the culture of Cork was to his father. It was a tender but critical experience of what fashioned his father to be the flawed man he was and of a city where John's friends told him what they thought he wanted to hear or what would be of advantage to themselves; bloody good honest Irishmen. Towards the end of their stay at the Victoria Hotel in the city James became wearied and dejected by his father's voice. The man John owned most money to was a Dublin solicitor Reuben J. Dodd who had a son in James' class in Belvedere. James' only defence was to rebuff this boy.

The next house move was to Millbourne Lane in Drumcondra near the river Tolka. This was decidedly downwards as their neighbours were working class people who resented the new 'middle class' arrival. This led to friction and even fist fights with the local boys. James himself had a fight with a boy at school but about his developing literary opinions. One of his essays was criticised by a teacher as containing heresy. His jealous classmates tackled him on the way home as to who was the greatest writer. James' nomination of Newman as the greatest prose writer brooked no opposition but his nomination of Byron as the best poet was vigorously opposed, as Byron was an evil man. When James would not recant they caught hold of him and beat him tearing his clothes. He went home crying but with his opinion intact.

In June 1895 James had completed two years in Belvedere and would have been expected to go into the next 'middle Grade'. But he did not do so. He was held back for a full years with the intention that he would surely come first in the examination the next year. But a factor was that he was too young for the examinations at Middle Grade. The year 1895-6 was a sort of scholastic interlude for the young Joyce[11]. It was always problematical to hold a pupil back for a year as he lost his place in one group and had to then establish it in the new group. But this does not appear to have caused young Joyce any such problems.

The fact that John Joyce [and his family] remained profligate, whenever possible, is clear when in 1894 James won a State prize in the Intermediate Examination of £20. John received the money and gave it to James to spend as he wished. He bought items for his siblings and took his parents to restaurants and to the theatre. This exercise was repeated as James won more prizes. Home life became more brutalised when shortly after the death of a new born baby, John drunk as usual, became violent at home and assaulted his wife on one occasion. The children had to come to the rescue with James jumping on his father's back as he tried to strangle his wife. A subsequent visit from the police had a calming effect on John. None of the children liked John, with Stanislaus being quite open about his detestation of his father.

The family's next house was at 17 North Richmond St in the inner city where the boys had briefly attended the Christian Brothers School. One of the neighbours, Eddie Boardman, became well-known as the owner of the first pneumatic-tired bicycle in the area. This was invented by Boyd-Dunlop of Belfast. James as the oldest boy in the

---

[11] . Sullivan Kevin, *Joyce Among the Jesuits* Columbia University Press 1958. p. 99-100

family was the centre of importance from his mother and especially his father. The next strongest character was Stannie, three years younger than James and prone to copy him. The girls were musical though second class citizens and fearful of their father. On Sundays John packed all the family off to Mass while staying home himself. In the afternoon John took the four boys walking through the city all the time telling stories and pointing out where famous people had lived. As a former rate collector he was full of stories about people. James had long come to accept his father and indulge his foibles, though Stan resented him. The family closest to the Joyces then were. Brendan Gallagher recalled James enjoying performing theatricals for visitors.

In Belvedere James soon began to distinguish himself through the breath of his reading and writing. He studied Latin, French and Italian. All the teachers liked him but especially the lay English teacher, George Stanislaus Dempsey, who would clearly display his pleasure on listening to him read his essays aloud on Mondays. The instinctive passion that the boy had for the English language was fostered and encouraged by this teacher[12].The other boys also liked James, especially when a blooper was made and he would hoot aloud in a mixture of agony and delight[13]. For an essay entitled '*My Favourite Hero*' he choose *Ulysses*. Other images that fascinated him were those of Parnell and Lucifer. When examination time came James studied intently as all the family afforded him space and quiet. In his second year he was lucky to be placed among the last group on 164th place and won a £20 exhibition payable for each of the next three years. The Dominicans offered him a free place at their boarding

[12] . Gorman Herbert, *James Joyce*, The Bodley Head 1941, p. 41.

[13] . Byrne JF. The Silent Years, *An Autobiography with Memoirs of James Joyce and Our Ireland*, Farrar, Straus and Young, New York 1953. p. 147.

school but James declined it, content to remain with the Jesuits, where he was already a *prima donna*. Despite being such an excellent model of a student James and Stan mitched from Belvedere on one occasion to spend the day wandering along the river Liffey towards the Pigeon House and Dublin Bay. The crowning events of his career at Belvedere came in 1895 when he became a member of the Sodality of the Blessed Virgin Mary and one year later he became the head. This was official recognition by the school authorities, which essentiality were about educating young Christians and hopefully selecting the best among them to become Jesuits. But though externally James appeared to be traversing such a path, internally he was developing a singular life separate from the values of Church and home and society. As with many young boys his interest in his sexuality was of paramount importance and the opposite sex became a never-ending fascination. This became centred in whatever was readily available. For James this came about with a maid with whom he had close physical encounter at home that came to the notice of the Jesuits. But a far more serious sexual encounter occurred along the canal bank when James was fourteen. He subsequently found it shameful and kept the experience to himself.

The rector at Belvedere, Fr. Henry, became suspicious of the impeccable James but was wary of challenging him directly. Instead he had an intimate talk with Stannie about himself but then began to question him about James. Stannie in awe of the rector, and in an attempt to end the inquisition, told him about the incident with the maid. Fr. Henry was very pleased to have his suspicions confirmed. He called in Mrs Joyce to say that her son James was inclined to evil ways. She was very upset. Stannie admitted that he been the informant. James laughed it off but Mrs Joyce blamed the maid who had already left. Mrs Joyce did not inform her husband but he surmised that something was amiss. James told him that there was a problem at school and that he should see the Rector. Fr. Henry only told John that his son James would give him trouble. John replied assuredly that he would not let him do so. James, who remained unflappable thought the episode, as became his wont, retained his position as head of the Sodality, though becoming further enmeshed in lustful images of sexuality.

The annual retreat that same year proved difficult for James as the powerful sermons made his sexual feelings number him among the beasts of the field. He was most unhappy and wished to repent and become pure again. The ritual of confession revivified him and he became mortified, prayerful and chaste. He prayed the Rosary on the way to school. This repentance lasted for about one year until he acknowledged that sexual continence was not possible for him and decided that the retreat and its aftermath had been unfair to him. The demands of the Catholic Church were too much and he could and would not obey them. His academic excellence improved as in 1897 he came 13th out of 49 and was awarded £30 for both succeeding years. He was the outstanding student in Belvedere, looked up to by his peers. He was a member of the library at Capel St. On one occasion the librarian warned his father that James was reading unsafe books. Around this period John had become involved in some casual work as a canvasser for advertisements in the *Freeman's Journal* and in preparing voting lists for local elections.

David Sheehy M.P. lived nearby at 2 Belvedere Place and held open house for musical evenings on Sundays. James and Stannie were regular attendees. Two of the Sheehy boys, Richard and Eugene, were at Belvedere. There were four Sheehy daughters, Hanna, Margaret, Mary and Kathleen, with James having a crush on Mary the youngest, though because of shyness being rather impolite with her[14]. James, though always keeping a physical distance from females, loved to sing at these evenings in his clear tenor voice and participate in their charades. When visiting females occasionally came into physical contact him, he froze. Richard Sheehy describes Joyce at this time, "*a tall slight stripling, with flashing teeth, plane blue eyes that sometimes had an icy look. He was fond of throwing back his head as he walked, and his mood alternated between cold, slightly haughty, aloofness and sudden boisterous merriment"*. Joyce acted in a play at the X.L. Café on Grafton St in March 1900 with Margaret Sheehy, of which she was the author. He played the main lead, a seductive villain. Mrs Joyce often came to the Sheehy's to accompany her son on the piano. *"I remember her as a frail, sad-faced and gentle lady whose skill at music suggested a sensitive, artistic temperament. She was very fond of James and he worshipped her"[15]*.

The next house move was to Windsor Tce in Fairview where the road stretched towards Clontarf and the Bull Wall. This house was owned by a clergyman named Love. Stannie Joyce hoped that this man had other sources of income, implying that the Joyce family did not pay rent but moved on after the current landlord ran out of tolerance. During his final year in Belvedere James acted as the headmaster in *Vice Versa* by F. Anstey and to the amusement of the audience, he took off the Rector who sat in the front row. An attempt by a priest in the school to encourage James to consider entering the Jesuits was

---

[14] . Donald Harman Akenson McGill Queens 1994 . p. 17-18. This information from Stanislaus Joyce in his Memoir is disputed by Peter Costello who argues that the lady in question was Emma Cleary, called 'E.C' in *Portrait* and spelled out as Emma Cleary in *Stephen Hero*. Akenson reinforces his theory quoting a letter James wrote to Stanislaus enquiring specifically about Maggie Sheehy. 7/2/1905 in Note 47. p. 493. Cf. also Costello Peter, *James Joyce The Years of Growth 1882-1915*, 1992. pp. 185-192.
[15] . Sheehy Eugene pp. 21-2

rebuffed as his passion for encounters with the female form had become paramount. Mrs Joyce would have been happy to have a son a priest but was not a woman to seek to exert any such influence[16]. Kevin Sullivan dates Joyce's first visit to a brothel at the age of fifteen years and eight months[17].

The Board of Education was responsible for the final examination in schools. It was a denominational body not concerned with any religious tests. Each school conducted its own religious examination. The Rector nominated the day before the State Examination for the religious examination in Belvedere. Three boys, including James, did not attend and the Rector was furious at this rebellion and bad example shown, particularly by the Head Boy. In a confrontation the next morning with the boys he told them that they would not be allowed to sit the State examination. The excuse they offered was that they were too busy studying. Another Jesuit teacher named Fr. MacErlaine intervened with the Rector, who relented and they were allowed to enter the exam hall late. James did not win an exhibition at this final exam though he did win a prize for English composition. As readers of James Joyce will recognise, many of these people, places and encounters figure in his writings, giving them a decidedly autobiographical quality.

---

[16] . Sullivan p. 124
[17] . ibid .p 125

Clongowes Wood School

Royal University St. Stephen's Green

CHAPTER 2

PRECOCIOUS UNIVERSITY STUDENT

'BLOOMING CENSORS'

1898-1904

James had begun to write poetry as a young teenager and to assemble the poems into collections, the first of which he called *Moods* and the second *Shine and Dark*. After attending a play called *Magda* by Hermann Sudermann with both his parents, James reported with confidence, but without brashness, that his family were experiencing the story-line of genius emanating within an unsuspecting family. James' literary interest at this early age became centred on Henrik Ibsen, who became one of the most dominant influences of his life. Ibsen came from a parochial background and was then aged seventy. Ibsen's motif was aloofness, artistic honesty, revelation, and exile from his own country. Ibsen became the counterpoint to Parnell in literary matters for the young student. James wore the ivy leaf commemorating Parnell on 6 October.

James became a university student at the Jesuit run Royal College on St Stephen's Green in September 1898. He may appear young, but sixteen and a half was not that unusual an age for university entrance. He became a member of the Sodality there and in 1901 became a member of the *Thomas Aquinas Society*. An example of how precociously startling he was, or possibly pretentious, even at that young age, is apparent in an essay he wrote on a painting of Christ by Munkacsy, in which he chided people who merely professed to be

Christian, "It *is grand, noble, tragic but it makes the founder of*

Christianity no more than a great social and religious reformer, a personality, of mingled majesty and power, a protagonist of a world-drama. No objection will be lodged against it on that score by the public, whose general attitude when they advert to the subject at all, is that of a painter, only less grand and less interested... Belief in the divinity of Christ is not a salient feature of secular Christianity. But occasional sympathy with the eternal conflict of truth and error, of right and wrong, as exemplified in the drama at Golgotha is not beyond its approval". WG Fallon reports that at University College Joyce continued to observe his religious duties, recalling that Joyce did *" attend to his religious duties. He was a member of the College sodality. This included going to confession and communion. He was also a member of St. Thomas Aquinas Academy"[18].*

James is second from left at rear.

[18] . O'Connor Ulick Ed. *The Joyce we Knew* Brandon 2004 p. 48-9.

Picture includes George Clancy, Constantine Curran, Seamus ClanDillon.

Where the money to pay his university fees came from is unclear but it appears likely that some relative came to the rescue, as his father was not in any position to do so. He made many good friends at university, three of whom were to die violently in 1916, George Clancy, Francis Sheehy Skeffington and Tom Kettle. His best friend was John Francis Byrne, who though two years older than James, had been at Belvedere with him. Byrne fascinated Joyce by out-doing him in cryptic taciturnity. Byrne was very ecclesiastical and ascetic in temperament[19]. He described James as '*thin, light and weak. Due to this, my attitude to him became, and to a great degree, remained protective*'[20]. Byrne played very long games of chess. James, who did not know one piece of chess from another, was often left waiting interminable for Byrne's company[21]. It was after one of those sessions that James first dubbed Byrne '*Cranley*' after a fourteenth century Archbishop of Dublin named Thomas Cranley. Byrne features in Portrait as the priest-like Cranley: "*how he had told Cranley of all the tumults and unrest and longings in his soul, day after day and night by night, only to be answered by his listening friend's listening silence…*". Byrne felt that James was jealous of the time he devoted to his chess partners. James documents this in *Stephen Hero* when he writes, *Cranley's chosen companions represented the rabblement in a stage of partial fermentation when it is midway between vat and flagon and Cranley seemed to please himself in the spectacle of this caricature of his own unreadiness*'. Byrne states that James valued

[19]. Gorman. p. 58.

[20]. Byrne JF. *The Silent Years*, Farrar, Straus and Young New York 1953. Pp. 40. 43, 53,54,61,

[21]. Byrne JF. ibid The name of the Chess Club was the Sackville Club. Among its members were Frank Sheehy-Skeffington, Eoin MacNeill and Arthur Griffith. Of the latter JF Byrne writes, "*the tenacious and devoted leader who won for his earthly reward the crown of martyrdom*" p. 187.

many words for their sounds and for their own sake as much as he did for their connotation. The meaning of the word or group of words often was less important for James than the word itself.

In those years James was moderately involved in physical exercise. He played handball occasionally, though his awkward style was akin to that of a rather un-athletic girl. He was a sprinter, very good in a short dash. He swam at the Bull Wall in Clontarf where all the youngsters sunbathed naked. His friend JF Byrne loved to go for long walks with little talking done. James was interested in talking but not in silent walking[22].

The author speaks at the National Library Ireland in 2014

---

[22] . Byrne JF. p. 176. JF Byrne recounts an amazing story that occurred around this time. Byrne saw a young man trying to end his life in the Liffey near Butt Bridge. Another young man riding by on his bicycle saw what was happening, jumped off his bicycle and into the river to rescue the man. He dragged the man out of the river and handed him over to a policeman and other bystanders. The rescuer then remounted his bicycle and cycled away without a word to anyone. Byrne identifies the rescuer as Oliver Gogarty. Gogarty would later save Arthur Griffith's life while swimming near the Joyce Tower off Bulloch Harbour.

The Reading Room at the NLI

Attendance at most lectures was optional and most scholarship took place in study and discussions at the National Library. The main reason for this was that Royal had virtually no library[23]. On one occasion as James sat down beside Byrne in the Library they engaged in discussion and as a loud howl from James echoed around the Reading Room the librarian expelled him from the Library. Joyce as usual excelled as a student in the university and as a poseur. He soon made his unique presence felt by writing excellent papers and overcoming contrary opinions even from within the academic staff. In May 1889 WB Yeats' play *The Countess Kathleen* was premiered. It had evoked great controversy before opening night, as heretical. It was met with great booing that night especially from some students in the audience. James applauded vigorously. A letter of protest for the *Freeman's Journal* against the play was circulated in the university

---

[23] Akenson p. 21.

the next morning by Francis Sheehy Skeffington. Byrne, Richard Sheehy and Kettle had also signed it. James was asked to sign it but refused. He refused to compromise for other people's feelings and had a distrust for crowd enthusiasms, religious or patriotic. He saw them all as fatal cages where the imprisoned will would die. For him self-integrity was fundamental[24].

The letter was published on 10 May and read, " *Sir, Mr. William Butler Yeats, as the most prominent among the founders of the Irish Literary Theatre, has at length fulfilled to his own satisfaction the contract concluded with the Irish public some months ago. But the terms of that contract, Mr. Yeats promised, if sufficiently supported, to 'put on the stage plays dealing with Irish subjects or reflecting Irish ideas and sentiments'. The drama in which Mr. Yeats claims to have satisfied at least one of these alternatives, 'The Countess Kathleen', has by this time acquired some notoriety. Two criticisms of the work, supported by extracts, have been generally circulated, that of Mr. O'Donnell and that of the 'Irish Daily Nation'. In replying to these criticism on Saturday, Mr. Yeats wisely confined himself to abstract platitudes, and sheltered himself behind an objection, which is in general valid, that a work cannot be fairly judged from mere quotation of words used by the personages who figure in that work. Let us sum briefly the results of our examination. The subject is not Irish. It has been shown that the plot is founded on a German legend. The characters are ludicrous travesties of the Irish Catholic Celt. The purpose of Mr. Yeats drama is apparently to show the sublimity of self-sacrifice, He represents the Irish peasant as a crooning barbarian, crazed with morbid superstition, who, having added the Catholic faith to his store of superstition, sells that faith for gold or*

---

[24]. Gorman p. 61.

bread in the proving of famine.

Is Mr Yeats prepared to justify this view of our national character?
Has Mr Yeats thoroughly considered the probable effect of presenting
this slanderous caricature of the Irish peasant?

We have no personal quarrel with Mr Yeats, we know him only from
his books. We recognise him as a fine literary artist. We recognise
him, further, as one endowed with a rare gift of extending an
infinitesimal quantity of the gold of thought in a seemingly infinite
area of the tinsel of melodious meaningless verse. We feel it our duty,
in the name of the honour of Dublin Catholic students of the Royal
University to protest against an art, even a dispassionate art, which
offers as a type of our people a loathsome brood of apostate"[25].

The *Literary and Historical Society* was founded by Cardinal
Newman in the Catholic University and continues in University
College Dublin to this day. Joyce used it as a vehicle for his literary
and dramatic exhibitions among his fellow students.

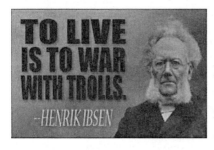

Henrik Ibsen remained one of his
heroes and on one occasion in his
second year a fellow student
named Arthur Clery declared *"The*
effect of Henrik Ibsen is evil". His

---

[25] . *Freeman's Journal* 10 May 1899.

mother then asked to read an Ibsen play as did his father. They both found it quite acceptable. James then wrote a long paper on Ibsen for delivery at the Society but it was initially censored by the President, Fr. Delaney. Joyce was later allowed deliver the paper. He argued, after St. Augustine, that an artist's concern is not to make his work religious or moral, beautiful or ideal, but to be truthful to fundamental laws; *"the sooner we understand our true position, the better; and the sooner then we will be up and doing on our way. Art, and chiefly drama, may help us to make our resting places with a greater insight and a greater foresight"[26]*. Many of his fellow students argued vigorously

against his views. *James replied to the debate and spoke for forty minutes without note dealing with each of his critics in turn. It was a masterful performance and delivered to the accompaniment of rounds of applause from the back benches.* After the debate had finished Seamus Clan Dillon expressed the view of many when he clapped Joyce vigorously on the back and exclaimed, 'Joyce, *that was magnificent but you're raving mad!"[27]*. JP Mahaffey a Provost of Trinity College later mourned that Joyce's writings proved that *"it was a mistake to establish a separate university for the aborigines of the island, for the corner-boys who spit into the Liffey"[28]*

James had earlier written to William Archer, editor of a literary magazine called the *Fortnightly Review* offering an article on Ibsen.

[26] . Ellmann Richard *The Critical Writings of James Joyce* Faber 1959. p. 46.

[27] . Sheehy Eugene p. 13.

[28] .O'Sullivan Michael, *Sean Lemass,* Dublin 1994 p. 55.

The editor declined but said he would consider a review of Ibsen's latest play *When We Dead Awaken*. Joyce succeeded in getting a French translation of the play and wrote a summary of it. He then argued passionately in favour of Ibsen's refusal to take on his critics, to remain above them, as Parnell had done and as James himself tended to do. The *Fortnightly Review* of 1 April 1900 published his article to the amazement of his fellow students. He received twelve guineas which pleased the family more so. But more acclamation arrived when the editor wrote to say that Ibsen himself had written to say *"I have read or rather spelt out, a review by Mr. James Joyce in the Fortnightly Review which is very benevolent and for which I should like to thank the author if only I had sufficient knowledge of the language"*. James replied, *"I wish to thank you for your kindness in writing to me. I am a young Irishman, eighteen years old, and the words of Ibsen I shall keep in my heart all my life.*
Jas A. Joyce 13 Richmond Avenue Fairview, Dublin April 28, 1900 "[29].

True to form James spent the money quickly. He gave his mother £1 and then took his father to London for a few days where they attended the theatre and met some editors. William Archer gave them lunch at the Royal Services Club.

John Joyce got a temporary job in Mullingar to work on the voting register. James and some of the family went with him. James wrote a play there called *A Brilliant Career* which alone among all his writings he made a dedication: *"To My own soul I dedicate the first true work of my life"*. He sent it to William Archer who replied that it interested yet puzzled him. He said it was too diffuse for the stage and

---

[29]. Ellmann. p. 74.

advised fewer characters. He remained unsure whether James had real talent but invited him to send more material to him. James replied that he did not like the play himself and later burned it.

James wrote to Ibsen in March 1901 to mark his seventy third birthday. He said:

8 *Royal Terrace Fairfield, Dublin*

Honoured Sir…how your wilful resolution to wrest the secret from life gave me heart, and how in your absolute indifference to public canons of art, friends and shibboleths you walked in the light of your inward heroism. Your work on earth draws to a close and you are near the silence. It is growing dark for you. I give you greeting—not humbly, because I am obscure and you in the glare, not sadly because you are an old man and I a young man, not presumptuously, nor sentimentally—but joyfully, with hope and with love, I give you greeting"[30].

James was very sparing in his praise of other writers. He admired George Meredith, Ibsen, Dante and James Clarence Mangan[31].

" *BLOOMING CENSORS*"

The Irish Literary Theatre of WB Yeats/Lady Gregory/Edward Martyn/George Moore, which had begun in May 1899, had provided a new outlet for Irish plays. Joyce had attended plays by Moore and Martyn in February 1900. WB Yeats had announced that they would perform continental plays in the future. Joyce had translated *Michael Kramer* by Gerhart Hauptmann and hoped to submit it for production. When he learned in October 1901 that the new season would again be

---

[30] . Gorman p. 70
[31] . Sheehy Eugene, p. 28.

of Irish plays, *'Twisting of the Rope'* by Douglas Hyde and a Yeats-George Moore version of the story of Diarmaid and Grania, he was furious. By surrendering to 'Irishness' Joyce believed that Yeats and his friends had compromised with the multitude and their theatre must be considered the property of the Rabblement of the most belated race in Europe...Henceforth his ironic and ambitious gaze was increasingly fixed on the continent[32]. He wrote a critical article, titled The *Day of the Rabblement,* for the College magazine, *St. Stephen's.* It began, *No man, said the Nolan, can be a lover of the true or the good unless he abhors the multitude; and the artist, though he may employ the crowd, is very careful to isolate himself...*[33]. His article was refused because of a reference to D'Annunzio's Il Fuoce, then on the *Index*. An appeal to the President Fr. Delaney failed. Joyce's friend Frank Skeffington had an article on womens' rights in the University rejected also. Joyce suggested that they publish both articles together themselves and distribute them. The Preface noted: *These two articles were commissioned by the Editor of St. Stephen's for that paper, but were subsequently refused insertion by the Censor. The writers are now publishing them in their original form, and each writer is responsible for what appears under his own name. F.J.C.S. J/A. J.".* They had 85 copies printed for £2.-5-0 on 21 October 1901. They distributed the pamphlet themselves. The only notice the pamphlet received was from Arthur Griffth's *United Irishman.* Its theatre critic, Frank Fay wrote that it contained "some grossly unjust assertions against the ILT...in a rather superior attitude Mr. Joyce sneers at Mr Yeats, Mr. George Moore & Mr Martyn; but sneering at these gentlemen has become so common that one wonders that Mr. Joyce would stoop so low...Patience, good Mr. Joyce and your desires for the masterpieces may have fulfilment. Surely the ILT and

---

[32] . Tobin Colm, *Penguin Book of Irish fiction pp xiii-xiv*
[33] . An original copy may be seen at the James Joyce Tower in Sandycove Dublin.

the Irish language both represent the fight of the minority against the 'damned compact majority'.

Griffith himself pinned a piece under his African nick name, *Cuagan,* supporting Joyce against censorship. *...because though it is written for a Catholic University Students' supposed organ, the censor – we grow censors in Ireland - refused it to be inserted...I have failed to find any heresy, blasphemy, immorality or sedition in this pamphlet...Mr. James Joyce writes on the ITL, and I do not agree with his criticism of it. But why the Censor strove to gag Mr. Joyce is to me as profound a mystery as to why we should grow Censors in this country. Turnips would be more useful. I hope this little pamphlet will have a large sale, if only to convince blooming censors that this is the twentieth century and that it is a holy and wholesome thing for men and women to use the minds God gave them and speak out the things they think"[34].*

Arthur Griffith

---

[34] . United Irishman 2/11/1901

Two Essays.

"A Forgotten Aspect of the University Question"

BY

F. J. C. SKEFFINGTON

AND

"The Day of the Rabblement"

BY

JAMES A. JOYCE.

PRICE TWOPENCE.

Printed by
GERRARD BROS.,
87 STEPHEN'S GREEN,
DUBLIN.

Joyce was thus first introduced to the Irish public by Griffith. Any young would-be writer would be grateful for this[35]. He graduated in October 1902 with a pass B.A. in Modern Languages, Latin and Logic. Together with several other graduates Joyce was offered a post of assistant professor at the University, which he declined in order not to be dependent of the Jesuits[36]. At the start of the new academic year he attended some medical lectures but in part due to financial pressures he decided to defer his medical studies and travelled to Paris on 3 December. He had already made a series of useful literary contacts in Dublin including WB Yeats, Lady Gregory and George Russell. He wrote to Lady Gregory, *I am going alone and friendless…into another country, and I am writing to you to know can you help me in any way*[37]. Yeats met him at Euston Station at six AM and entertained him for the day introducing him to useful contacts. Joyce went on to Paris overnight and stayed at the Hotel Corneille. He made an abortive attempt to see Maud Gonne but she was unavailable. She wrote to him explaining, *"I was very sorry not to see you when you called last evening. The polite lie about my being in bed was diplomacy on the part of my concierge as at such an early hour I never retire to rest…"*. Though Gonne gave him another appointment he decided not to keep it[38].

---

[35] . Sheehy Eugene, *May it please the Court,* CJ Fallon . 1951 p. 35. Miss Sylvia Beach had never heard of this article until many years later Hanna Sheehy-Skeffington presented her with some copies in her bookshop in Paris and insisted on paying for them.

[36] . Sullivan p. 224

[37] . ibid. p. 226

[38] ' Jordan Anthony J. *Arthur Griffith with James Joyce & WB Yeats – Liberating Ireland* Westport 2013 . 57-8.

Maud, baby Seaghan, John MacBride.

He began writing book reviews for the Dublin *Daily Express* on 4 December, the first of which was a book of poetry commemorating the recently deceased Willie Rooney. The book was published by Griffith as a tribute to his friend, mentor and avatar. Joyce embarked on his sole criterion of literary truth, wrote a devastating review, insulting to Griffith and the entire nationalist movement, for the Dublin *Daily Express*. He said, *an examination of the poems and ballads of William Rooney does not warrant one in claiming for them any high honours... Little is achieved in these verses, because the writing is so careless, and is so studiously mean...They were written it seems, for a paper and societies week after week and bear witness to some desperate and weary energy. But they have no spiritual and living energy, because they come from one in whom the spirit is in a manner dead, or at least in its own hell, a weary and foolish spirit, speaking of redemption and revenge, blaspheming against tyrants and going forth full of tears and curses, upon its infernal labours*[39].

Griffith, grievously wounded, retorted by reissuing Joyce's review as an advertisement in the following week's *United Irishman*. When Joyce had written that Rooney "*might have written well if he had not*

---

[39] . Daily Express 11/12/1902.

suffered from one of those big words which make us so unhappy",
Griffith added the missing word "*patriotism*".

Joyce then enrolled in medical school. He was very positive for a
brief period but when he discovered that fees must be paid in cash and
without delay, he could not continue[40]. He became ill due to the cold
and a poor diet and induced his mother to insist he return home for
Xmas and to send him money for the fare. He stayed for a month and
met Oliver Gogarty and played the visiting Parisian student role. On
his return journey he again stopped in London and met several literary
contacts. He got some reviewing work but soon was sending begging
letters home. One successful job he succeeded in was to get an
interview with Henri Farman about the Gordon Bennett Cup Races
and sell it to the *Irish Times*.

JM Synge   St. Stephen's Green opposite Royal College

JM Synge arrived in March 1903 to stay at Hotel Corneille. They

---

[40] . Gorman p. 90.

spent most of their time together arguing. Synge showed the manuscript of his *Riders to the Sea* to Joyce who described one act plays as "*dwarf drama*". Joyce survived in Paris for a few months hand to mouth, earnings from reviewing, teaching English, borrowing from acquaintances, frequenting brothels. He visited Tours, attended Vespers and Mass at Notre Dame. On the night 10 April he got a telegram, "*Mother Dying Come Home Father*' He borrowed the fare home from one of his language students. Joyce's mother was extremely important to James, yet when she asked him to go to Confession and Holy Communion; he refused to moderate his beliefs to please her even as she was dying. The furthest he would go was to acknowledge belief in a Supreme Being. Responding to entreaties from his Aunt Josephine Murray who tended to May Joyce during her long illness, to follow his mother's wishes, he declared that he was following the example of Saint Aloysius Gonzaga and Jesus Christ himself who refused his mother's wishes[41]. He had depended on her approval for vindication most of all while living in Paris. At home he played the piano and sang for her. Mrs Joyce did not die easily but lingered for several months. James continued to play the returned Parisian idling about town while his father once more mortgaged his house to pay the medical expenses. As his wife continued to weaken her husband began to drink more and create a nuisance at home. On one occasion his usual disgraceful behaviour outdid itself as he screamed at his wife and the dour Stanislaus went to attack him. Mrs Joyce tried to get out of bed and James had to come between his father and his brother. He ejected John and locked him into another room from which he escaped through a window. At last May Joyce died on 13 August 1903. James and Stanislaus refused to kneel as the family said prayers around the bed. As the youngest daughter cried

---

[41] . Byrne JF. *Silent Years,* Farrar Straus and Young New York 1953 p. 86-7

aloud, James consoled her saying that *"Mother is in heaven. She is far happier now than she has ever been on earth"*.

James began to write book reviews again for the *Daily Express* at thirty shillings each until he had a row with the editor. He tried to get a job in the National Library and turned down a job teaching French at University College. He considered setting up a newspaper with Sheehy Skeffington but was unable to raise the capital required. He told his Aunt Josephine that *"I want to be famous while I am alive"*[42]. The Joyce household deteriorated further after May's death often with little to eat in the crumbling house. The family consisted of three sons James, Stanislaus, Charles and six daughters Margaret, May, Florence, Eileen, Eva and Mabel.

Amid this desolation James wrote the first version of his own life, *A Portrait of the Artist as a Young Man* as a paper for the newly founded journal *Dana.* It was rejected on the basis of opaqueness and sexual explicitness[43].One of the editors, John Eglinton who worked in the National Library wrote of Joyce, " *He observed me silently as I read, and when I handed it back to him with the timid observation that I did not care to publish what was to myself incomprehensible, he replaced it silently in his pocket"*. Joyce's brother Stanislaus commented, *"The paper was rejected by the editors, Fred Ryan and W. Magee [real name of John Eglinton]. Jim thinks they rejected it because it was all about himself...Jim is beginning his novel, as he usually begins things, half in anger, to show that in writing about himself he has a subject of more interest than their aimless discussion...A title of mine was accepted: Stephen Hero, from Jim's own name in the book Stephen Dedalus"*.

---

[42] . Ellmann Richard *James Joyce* Oxford 1983 p. 142.
[43] . Eglinton John *Irish Literary Portraits 1935.* p. 136

James also began writing poetry during the summer of 1904 all the while enjoying the company of his friends Gogarty, Sheehy Skeffington and Mary Sheehy whom he admired from a distance. She thought him very wicked as he responded "*I do my best*". His brother Stanislaus, who was devoted to James, had, to his father's horror, given up his employment and joined James as a drunken lay-about. James had entered the *Feis Ceoil* in 1903 as a tenor and determined to do the same in 1904. The family piano had long been sold so he decided to move out and hire a grand piano from Piggott's. He also took singing lessons from Vincent O'Brien who had worked with John McCormack. The *Feis Ceoil* took place on 16 May where he sang a song from *The Prodigal Son* and *A Long Farewell.* He was then required to sing a piece from sight but refused and walked off. He was awarded a bronze medal by default and resisted offers of free professional training. He gave his medal to Aunt Josephine.
James then taught briefly at the private Clifton School in Dalkey. It features in U*lysses* where '*Mr Deasy*' is the Headmaster.

James had a strange relationship with Oliver Gogarty. They were rarely seen then without the other[44].They were two prima donnas constantly hopping off each other with neither willing to doff the cap to the other. Gogarty was fairly well-off and James was the shabbily dressed, penniless, lewd-spoken youth whose disrespectability was striking because of the witticisms that rose out of it[45]. He tried regularly to borrow money and goods from Gogarty who was a medical student in Oxford during 1904. He kept inviting James to visit where he would put him up. Gogarty wisely refused to pay his travel costs, fearing that Joyce would not come and spend his money. James could not even pay the rent for his room and on 15 June had to

---

[44] .Colum Mary & Colum Padraig, *Our Friend James Joyce*, Gollancz 1959. P. 39
[45] . ibid p. 45.

leave. He was taken in by Gretta and James Cousins at 22 Dromard Ave in Sandymount.

 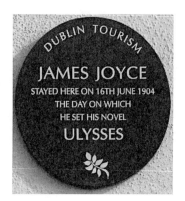

NORA BARNACLE

A few days earlier on 10 June Joyce had met an animated woman on Nassau St who responded joyfully to his greeting. She worked in nearby *Finn's Hotel* on Leinster St and lived in. They chatted for a time and she agreed to meet him on 14 June at the corner of Merrion Square in front of Wilde's house. She told him her name was Nora Barnacle and she was from Galway. James duly turned up at the appointed place but Nora did not appear. He wrote her a short note:

60 Shelbourne Road

I may be blind. I looked for a long time at a head of reddish-brown hair and decided it was not yours. I went home quite dejected. I would

like to make an appointment but it might not suit you. I hope you will
be kind enough to make one with me—if you have not forgotten me!

James A Joyce

15 June 1904[46]

Nora replied immediately. They met on 16 June and went to Ringsend
for a walk where she demonstrated her worldly experience by
performing a manual sexual exercise on him[47]. Nora was a West of
Ireland Catholic woman, sexually active, with a quick turn of phrase
and a sharp wit. She was born in 1884 and raised by her Grandmother
on her mother's side, Catherine Healy at St Augustine St. Her father,
a baker whom Nora liked, was a heavy drinker whose wife expelled
him from the family home[48]. The main man in her young life was her
Uncle Patrick Healy, whose brother worked in the British Civil
service. Nora attended the local Convent of Mercy leaving school
aged twelve to become a porter at the Presentation Convent. Nora
thus lived near both her parents in Galway, but apart from them. She
developed as an independent-minded young city woman who had
several boyfriends including Michael Furey, before she came to
Dublin. James' reaction was to fall head over heels in love with Nora,
despite unwelcome comments from his brooding brother Stanislaus
and his friends Gogarty and Cosgrave. They met frequently during the
following days as he analysed minutely what was happening to him.
They had much family history in common and she was the complete
antidote to his devastation in losing his mother. Yet he did not change
quickly but continued to drink heavily and make a nuisance of

[46] . Letters 11 p. 42. Future quotations from Joyce Letters in the text are not foot-noted.

[47] . Stewart Bruce, *A Short Literary Life of James Joyce* in, Latham Sean Ed. *James Joyce*, IAP 2010.p. 28

[48] . Maddox Breda *Nora A Biography of Nora Joyce*, Hamish Hamilton1988

himself. Mary Colum who later met Nora in Paris and described her as 'not only beautiful but vivacious and humorous'[49].

On 20 June James arrived drunk at a rehearsal of the National Theatre Society in Camden St, collapsed in the dark passage way and frightened the actresses making their way in. He was ejected by the Fay brothers, George Roberts and Seumas O'Sullivan. This incident features in *Ulysses*[50]. Around the same time he approached a lady in St Stephens Green not realising she was escorted. This man assaulted Joyce. Nevertheless Nora, to the surprise of all, was becoming very important if not essential to James. In August he had an invitation to sing at the Ancient Concert Rooms on Brunswick St with John McCormack. He organised his friend Cosgrave to escort Nora there. She was highly impressed as he appeared to sing for her, '*In Her Simplicity*' and '*My Love is from a Far Countree*'. She believed that he could make a living through his singing. All this time he was writing and publishing poetry occasionally referring to Nora as his '*companion*'.

James felt that he had to tell Nora the kind of life he lived, his sexual exploits, his rejection of Christianity, his father's ill treatment of his mother and the family through drinking, how only one of his many siblings understood him, how he cared nothing for the others, how he was a vagabond, a beggar. He wrote, " *My mind rejects the whole present social order and Christianity- home, the recognised virtues,classes of life and religious doctrines…Six years ago I left the catholic Church, hating it most fervently. I found it impossible for me to remain in it on account of the impulses of my nature. I made secret war upon it when I was a student and declined to accept the positions*

[49]. Colum Mary & Colum Padraig, Our Friend James joyce CJ Fallon 1951. P. 114.
[50]. *Ulysses* Wordwell 1987. p. 195. This is an example of how Joyce constantly used biographical facts even when they cast him in a poor light.

it offered me. By doing this I made myself a beggar but I retained my pride. Now I make open war upon it by what I write and say and do" He then remarkably referred to a particular physical intimacy that occurred between them, saying "I *however consider it a kind of sacrament and the recollection of it fills me with amazed joy"*. He confessed that he wore a mask like everyone else, adding *"Certain people who know that we are much together often insult me about you"*. He told her that *"no human being ever stood so close to his soul as you stand, it seems, and yet you can treat my words with painful rudeness"*. This must have been very difficult for Nora to comprehend or tolerate but she felt he was posing somewhat and her attitude to him challenged him in a way any others had not.

It was on 11 September 1904 that Joyce wrote another remarkable letter to Nora. It reads;

The Tower Sandycove

My Dear Nora,

I suppose you have been very much upset since last night. I will not speak of myself for I feel as if I had acted very cruelly. In a way I have no right to expect that you should regard

*me as anything more than the rest of men – in fact in view of my own
life I have no right at all to expect it. But yet I seemed to have
expected it if only because I myself had never regarded anyone as I
regarded you. There is also something a little devilish in me that
makes me delight in breaking down peoples ideas of me and proving
to them that I really am selfish, proud, cunning and regardless of
others. I am sorry that my attempt last night to act according to what
I believed to be right should have caused you so much pain but I do
not see how I could have acted otherwise. I wrote you a long letter
explaining as well as I could how I felt that night and it seemed to me
that you were fretting about what I said and treating me as if I were
simply a casual comrade in lust. You will perhaps object to the
brutality of my words but, believe me, to treat me as that is, so far as
my attitude towards you is concerned, to dishonour me. Surely to God
you are a woman and can understand what I say! I know that you
have acted very nobly and generously to me but try and answer my
frankness. Above all do not go about brooding as it will make you ill
and you know that you are in delicate health. Perhaps you will be
able to send me a line tonight to say that you can forgive me for all
the pain I have caused you.*

Jim

11 September 1904[51].

James had decided that autobiographical fiction was to be his career
and decided that he had to move far away from the *'trolls'* surrounding
him. The continent and not England where so many Irish writers
settled, beckoned him again, alone or with Nora? He sounded out his

---

[51] . A copy of this letter may be seen at the Joyce Tower at Sandycove Dubin.

close friend JF Byrne on whether he should ask her to accompany him, in his impecunious state, and whether she would accept? Under questioning Joyce came close to admitting that he '*loved*' Nora in a way he never felt about any other woman. He said, '*Honestly, Byrne, there's not another girl in the world I could ever love as I do Nora*'. Byrne then advised him to put the question to Nora: "*Don't wait, and don't hesitate. Ask Nora, and if she agrees to go away with you, take her*'[52]. James told Nora of his plans and by way of a proposal he asked her if there was anybody who understood him? She replied in affirmation. She had made her mind up about him and anything else followed naturally. He was filled with pride and joy for her love as he excoriated the lack of honesty or naturalness in the social life in Ireland. She wished him to be more clear about his love for her and was not satisfied with declarations of '*fondness and desire*' until he wrote about '*my love or affection for you*'. James then spoke to his father of his plan of leaving Ireland again, without mentioning Nora. John agreed that it was the right thing to do.

James then began to explore employment at a Berlitz school in Europe. He contacted publishers about a poetry collection. He wrote to WB Yeats asking for the return of plays he had written. Yeats could not '*help you with money*'. Lady Gregory sent him £5. Most other financial requests failed. Stanislaus and Aunt Josephine went to the boat at the North Wall to see James and Nora off to Paris on 9 October. They were two single people aged twenty and twenty two and among 37,413 Irish people who emigrated that year. It was only much later that John Joyce discovered that a woman had accompanied his son.

---

[52] . Byrne JF. *Silent Years* 1935. p. 148.

CHAPTER 3

Émigré Teacher & Writer at Pola & Trieste

The couple arrived penniless in Paris. James left Nora in a park near where their boat-train had arrived while he tried to contact friends to borrow for the onward journey to Zurich. They arrived in Switzerland on 11 October and went to Gasthuas Hoffnung where they made love for the first time. Despite assurances there was a job for James at the Berlitz School in Zurich, this was wrong. The employment agency that had dispatched him on this wild-goose chase was a swindle[53]. The Director of the School, who had never heard of his name, told him of a post in Trieste to where James and Nora travelled, arriving on 20 October. On arrival there, as he had done in Paris, James left Nora in the park while he walked into town to make arrangements for the night. At the Piazza Grade he got involved with drunken English sailors and all were arrested and jailed. He got the English Consul to come and arrange his release as an innocent party in the escapade[54]. James was not impressed by the bureaucratic attitude of the English Consul. There was no post for him at the Berlitz School again and he lived by his wits, borrowing continuously. The superior of the Trieste school, Artifoni, had just opened a new school at Pola about 150 miles south of Trieste. He created a post there for James and the couple left on the four hour boat journey along the Istrian coast to Pola. Artifoni met them and advised that they act officially as a

---

[53] . Gorman Herbert *James Joyce, a Definitive Biography* London 1941.

[54] . McCourt John, *The Years of Bloom, James Joyce in Trieste 1904-1920,* the Lilliput Press 2000 p.8-9.

married couple. Austria was a Catholic country. James' university degree entitled him to use the title of '*Dr*'. All the while during these erratic days James was continuing to write *Dubliners*. The Deputy Principal at the Berlitz School was a man named Francini with whom Joyce had much in common and they became good friends, as did Nora with his wife. Later the Francinis invited them to share their house, where James' piano playing and singing were well regarded. Clotilde Francini was Florentine and became Nora's tutor in cookery, fashion and Italian. The energetic sexual encounters between the lovers, to the thrill of both parties, made Nora pregnant in October. James requested his Aunt Josephine Murray to write and tutor Nora on midwifery. He corresponded almost daily with Stanislaus who was his literary keeper. On 3/12 1904 he told Stan that *"Nora's father is a baker…She has had many love-affairs, one when quite young with a boy who died"*. He told his brother that Nora was uninterested in his literary output. Stanislaus was critical of Nora but despite the enormous difficulties in their lives, James praised Nora, writing *"I admire her and I love her and I trust her- I cannot tell how much"*. He told Aunt Josephine that Nora trusted him. All the while he was sending the latest chapters of his '*Stephen Hero-Portrait of the Artist*' to Stanislaus for criticism. He was reading extensively, including several lives of Christ. He did not particularly like Pola, describing it as a '*back-of-God-speed place*' and was quite happy in March 1905 to transfer to the Berlitz School at 32 via San Nicolo in Trieste, where he and Nora would live for the next ten years. The fact that the Francinis also came back to Trieste was a bonus. To make ends meet Nora began to take in washing.

The Berlitz School

Trieste had similarities with Dublin but offering a much greater choice of music, opera and drama. It had two opera houses, severable theatres, two large concert halls and twenty one cinemas[55] It had a large population, mostly Italian, but was ruled for centuries by the Austrian Empire. Many favoured a break with Austria. James wrote Stan on 12 /7 '05, "Trieste *is the rudest place I have ever been in...Nora is afraid to go out in the street*".

James poked fun at Maud Gonne, her husband and Arthur Griffith, writing to Stan in March 1905, "I *have read in the Figaro of the divorce of the Irish Joan of Arc from her husband, Pius the Tenth. I*

---

[55] . Price Stanley, *James Joyce and Italo Svedo,* Somerville Press 2016. p.19.

suppose will alter Catholic regulations to suit the case: an Italian comment says Irish genius is not domestic. Poor little U.I. indignant chap!"[56].

The local newspaper *Ill Piccolo della Sera*, owned by a Hungarian Jew favoured Italian nationalism. The editor Roberto Prezioso began to learn English with Joyce. Joyce's salary was quite reasonable but for an avowed socialist his lifestyle began to favour more expensive tastes and he reverted to regular borrowing. He also entered several schemes to make money including becoming an agent for Foxford rugs in Trieste and another following his father's example of doing magazine puzzles in the hope of winning monetary prizes. He told Stanislaus that he was missing Dublin, *"a slice of boiled leg of mutton with turnips and carrots"*; Nora wanted to see *"a kettle on the hob"*. He thought of getting a cottage outside Dublin. Why should he expose himself to a *"degrading exile"* to convince others that *"I was a person of talent"?* All he wanted from life, he told Stanislaus, was to be able to *"write tiny little sentences about the people who betrayed me and sent me to hell"*.

The birth of his son, Georgio, in July 1905, nine months and sixteen days to their first love making in Zurich, made Joyce happy. There was to be no baptism then, though this occurred, unknown to James in 1912 in Dublin. James told his sister that the most important thing that can happen to a man is the birth of a child. The baby was called Georgio in memory of James' brother George who had died. Nora called him Georgie.

Before James completed *Dubliners* he had his amanuensis Stanislaus

---

[56] . Jordan Anthony J. *The Yeats/Gonne/MacBride Triangle*, Westport Books 2000 p. 16. Joan of Arc refers to Maud Gonne while Pius X refers to her husband Major John MacBride. They engaged in a bitter divorce case in Paris in 1905-6 over the custody of their baby, Sean MacBride. James' father had been one of the contributors to the Irish Transvaal Committee which had supported MacBride's Brigade during the Anglo- Boer War.

check various details for accuracy. He wrote Stan on 19 July 1905, *"The Dublin papers will object to my stories as to a caricature of Dublin life. Do you think there is any truth in this?"* George Roberts of Maunsel Publishers in Dublin, with whom James had several earlier contacts, was interested in publishing the book. But James, who needed money, thought that a London publication could be more beneficial. He therefore sent it to Grant Richards of London on 3 December 1905 and so began his *'Calvary'* of trying to get published.

James had earlier tried to get Stanislaus to come to Trieste. When an immediate vacancy came up in the Berlitz in Trieste he told him of the vacancy. Stanislaus, aged twenty, decided to take up the offer, despite the fact that he knew James was using him for his own purposes. But Stanislaus was, and wanted to continue to be, part of his brother's great enterprise. He left Dublin on 20 October 1905. One of the first things James did when Stanislaus arrived was to try to borrow money from him. Stanislaus was a very different character to James. He was a rigid atheist without many of the subterfuges necessary for sociability. He did not approve of James lifestyle, dining out all the time, drinking, borrowing money, arguing with Nora, long silences. He realised that his brother did not display domesticated traits and saw himself as an artist who believed and certainly acted as if the world owed him a living. Stanislaus also saw James as a genius and wanted to be a part of it. James began to have doubts about Nora and thought she had become indifferent to him. He entertained thoughts of leaving her but Stanislaus reprimanded him over his appalling drunken behaviour. The Joyces moved in to live with the Francinis as they had done in Pola and this worked well.

Trieste

On 2 March 1905 James had written Stanislaus, *"The English teacher says I will die a Catholic because I am always moping in and out of the Greek Churches and am a believer at heart, whereas in my opinion I am incapable of belief of any kind"*.

James' frustrations increased in 1905 on the literary front as his collection of poetry, *Chamber Music*, was turned down by several London publishers. He was more successful the following year when he got a contract from Grant Richards for the publication of *Dubliners*. Joyce sent an additional story for the collection which Grant Richards gave to his printer without reading it. The printer, who was liable like the publisher for libellous material, indicated that there were several doubtful passages in several of the stories. Several tortured months passed as writer and publisher negotiated revisions of texts.

In late 1905 James wrote to Aunt Josephine saying that relations between himself and Nora were not good. He was jealous that she *"does not seem to make much difference between me and the rest of the men she has known and I can hardly believe that she is justified in this. I am not a very domestic animal—after all I suppose I am an artist"*.

UNHAPPY SOJURN IN ROME

In May the Berlitz School was not able to employ both Joyces over the slack summer months. James, always eager for a change of scenery, was happy to leave Trieste and applied for and got a job in a bank in Rome as an English language clerk. Among his references was a letter from the Lord Mayor of Dublin, Tim Harrington, written for him in 1902 as he was leaving Dublin. Nora, James and Georgio arrived in the eternal city on 31 July 1906. Despite its reputation so loved by so many famous writers, Rome and the Italians did not impress James, nor did his fellow employees in the bank. The oppressive summer heat did not help. Though his pay was good, the hours went from 7.30 AM to 8.30 P.M. and he was soon trying to borrow from Stanislaus who was trying to pay off James' Triestean debts. James succeeded in getting a loan from the English Consul in Rome. He decided to start offering English lessons in his room after work, though that necessitated Nora and Georgio having to vacate it until ten o'clock. His landlady soon locked him out and the family had to stay in a hotel for a few nights. When they next got rooms they had to share a bed for the first time and did so lying in opposite directions. He told his students, "I *like Papal Rome because it makes me think of that pig of a Pope, Alexander VI, in the arms of his mistress and daughter Lucrezia Borgia"*. Neither James or Nora made any close friends in Rome.

James was a voracious reader and eager especially for anything coming out of Ireland. On 12 August 1906 he wrote Stan, "*I sent you today Sinn Fein with two marked paragraphs [dialogue of the Day' by Shanganagh [a Parody of FS Skeffington's weekly column].* He was very critical to Stanislaus of books by George Moore, Seumas O'Kelly and Tom Kettle. He admitted that his relationships with men were difficult and unrewarding for him, except that of Stanislaus, whom he told, *"On the other hand two ill-equipped women, to wit,*

Aunt Josephine and Nora, seem to be able to get at my point of view, and if they do not get on with me as well as they might, they certainly manage to preserve a certain loyalty which is very commendable and pleasing". He and Stanislaus agreed generally on most things except James' socialism and the Irish Parliamentary Party policy at Westminster, one of whose proponents was his old friend Tom Kettle. James surprised his brother by vehemently rejecting the policy of moderation including the sending of Irish parliamentarians to London at all. He reported to Stan on 4 Oct 1906, *"I went also to Wyndham. He hates Rome. He says that talking to Alderman Kelly and the union jack that the Irish are very disloyal. He has a union jack furled in his hat. I argued with him politely for an hour then left".* He asked Stan, *"Does Aunt Josephine write to you? She never writes to me and sends Sinn Fein at long intervals. Is there nobody in Ireland who will think it worth their while to make a bundle of any old paper and send them on to me?"* *Sinn Fein* became James' chief source of current and historical events in Ireland and was to make him become a radical Irish separatist from its unjust coloniser, England. Unknown to Stanislaus, James had become an ardent follower of Arthur Griffith and the policies he advocated in the organisation he founded in 1905 – *Sinn Fein*, meaning *Ourselves Alone!*[57] James felt reasonably that when a man of the stature of Parnell had failed to succeed in having a parliament restored to Dublin, the likes of Tom Kettle was unlikely to succeed. He wrote Stan on 9 October 1906 from Rome, *"[Arturo] Labriola spoke yesterday, the paper says, with extraordinary rapid eloquence for two and a half hours. He reminds me of Griffith. He*

---

[57] . In *Ulysses* the name *Sinn Fein* occurs 12 times and the *United Irishman* 10 times.

attacked the intellectuals and the parliamentary socialists. He belongs or is leader of the Syndicalist".

James told Stanislaus on 25 September 1906 that the *United Irishman* was the only paper in Ireland worth reading: *In my opinion Griffith's speech at the meeting of the National Council justifies the existence of his paper. He probably has to lease out his columns to scribblers like Gogarty and Column, and virgin martyrs like his sub-editor. But so far as my knowledge of Irish affairs goes, he [Griffith] was the first person in Ireland to revive the separatist idea on modern lines nine years ago. He wants the creation of an Irish consular service abroad, and of an Irish bank at home. What I don't understand is that apparently while he does the talking and the thinking, two or three fatheads like Martyn and Sweetman don't begin either of the schemes...A great deal of his [economic] programme perhaps is absurd but at least it tries to inaugurate some commercial life for Ireland and to tell the truth once or twice in Trieste, I felt myself humiliated when I heard the little Galatti girl sneering at my impoverished country. You may remember that on my arrival in Trieste I actually took some steps to secure an agency for Foxford tweeds there. What I object to most of all in his paper is that it is educating the people of Ireland on the old pap of racial hatred whereas any one can see that if the Irish question exists, it exists for the Irish proletariat chiefly. On the whole I don't think it fair to compare him with a stupid mountebank like knickerbockers (F. Sheehy-Skeffington).*

When Stanislaus wrote that Griffith feared the Church too much to achieve anything significant, James agreed writing, "*I quite agree with you that Griffith is afraid of the priests –and he has every reason to be so. But possibly they are also a little afraid of him too. After all, he is holding out some secular liberty to the people and the Church doesn't approve of that. I quite see, of course that the Church is still, as it was in the time of Adrian IV, the enemy of Ireland; but I think her time is almost up. For either Sinn Fein or Imperialism will conquer the present Ireland. If the Irish Programme did not insist on the Irish language I suppose I could call myself a nationalist. As it is I am content to recognise myself as an exile; and, prophetically, a repudiated one".*

As Stanislaus criticised some of the contributors to the *United Irishman*, James replied astutely, *"you complain of Griffith using Gogarty & Co. How do you expect him to fill his paper; he can't write it all himself. The part he does write, at least, has some intelligence and directness about it. As for O.G., I am waiting for the Sinn Fein policy to make headway in the hope that he will join it, for no doubt whatever exists in my mind but that if he gets the chance and the moment comes, he will play the part of MacNally & Reynolds. I do not say this out of spleen. It is my final view of his character; a very native growth, and if I begin to write my novel again, it is in this way I shall treat them. If it is not far-fetched to say that my action, and that of men like Ibsen & etc is a virtual intellectual strike, I would call such people as Gogarty and Yeats and Colm the blacklegs of literature. Because they have tried to substitute us, to serve the old idols at a lower rate, when we refused to do so for a higher...Irish intellectuals are tiresome".*

When Joyce read Gogarty's article on 'venereal excess in Griffith's *Sinn Fein*, he was infuriated, writing to his brother;

"Anyway, my opinion is that if I put down a bucket into my own soul's well, sexual department, I draw up Griffith's and Ibsen's and Skeffington's and Bernard Vaughan's and St. Aloysius' and Shelley's and Renan' water along with my own". He then gives a preview of

the kind of material in Ulysses which would so shock, adding *"And I am going to do that in my novel [inter alia] and plank the bucket down before the shades and substances above mentioned to see how they like it; and if they don't like it I can't help them. I am nauseated by their lying drivel about pure men and pure women and spiritual love for ever; blatant lying in the face of truth... Perhaps my view of life is too cynical but it seems to me that a lot of this talk about love is nonsense. A woman's love is always maternal and egotistic. A man, on the contrary side by side with his extraordinary cerebral sexualism and bodily fervour [from which women are normally free] possesses a fund of genuine affection for the 'beloved' or 'once beloved' object...".*

You ask me what I would substitute for parliamentary agitation in Ireland. I think the Sinn Fein policy would be more effective. Of course I see that its success would be to substitute Irish for English capital but no one I suppose denies that capitalism is a stage for progress. The Irish proletariat has yet to be created. A feudal peasantry exists; scraping the soil but this would with a national revival or with a definite preponderance of England surely disappear."

James acknowledged that capital was necessary before socialism had a chance to be created.

JOYCE'S RELIGION

Elizabeth Bowen wrote of Joyce, "He *was reared and educated in a religion from which a deep nature does not without crisis secede and from which a lonely nature dreads to detach itself"*[58]. Though James Joyce appeared to be viciously anti-Catholic it was and remained an integral part of his culture from which he could not escape. His writings are full of Catholicism. There are literally hundreds of references to the Old and New Testaments of the Bible in his *Ulysses*[59]. *Portrait of the Artist as a Young Man* is also subsumed by his struggle with Catholicism. In *Portrait* he enters into a dialogue with his best friend Cranley on the matter.

Joyce [Stephen]: *"I had an unpleasant quarrel this evening with my mother, about religion...She wishes me to make my easter duty...I will not....I will not serve..."*

Cranley , *Do you believe in the Eucharist?*

Joyce, *""I do not. I neither believe nor disbelieve in it...I do not wish to overcome them.*

Cranley, *"It is a curious thing how your mind is supersaturated with the religion in which you say you disbelieve.*

Joyce, *"I did believe in it at school.*

Cranley: *" Do you love your mother?*

Joyce; *I don't know what your words mean.... I tried to love God.*

Cranley: *Would you not try to save her from suffering more even if...or would you?*

---

[58] Bowen Elizabeth, *The Weight of a World of Feeling, Reviews and Essays by Elizabeth Bowen. Ed by Allan Hepburn Northwestern University Press, 2016*

[59] . In *Ulysses*, there are 248 references to the Old Testament and 186 to the New Testament. Jesus features 64 times, Mary 47, Mary Magdalen 3, Angelus 2, Anti-Christ 4 and Mass Ceremonies 53.

Joyce; *If I could, that would cost me very little.*
Cranley: *Then do so. Set her mind at rest. Whatever else is unsure in this stinking dunghill of a world a mother's love is not. Your mother brings you into this world, carries you first in her body. What do we know what she feels? But whatever she feels, it, at least, must be real. It must be. What are our ideas our ambitions? Play. Ideas! Why, that bloody bleating goat Temple has ideas..*

Joyce *"Jesus, too, seems to have treated his mother with scant courtesy in public". I am not at all sure that Jesus was not the son of God. He is more like a son of God than a son of Mary*

Cranley: *Then you do not intend to become a protestant?*

Joyce: *I said that I had lost the faith but not that I had lost self-respect. What kind of libertarian would that be to forsake an absurdity which is logical and coherent and to embrace one which is illogical and incoherent? Probably I shall go away...I will not serve that in which I no longer believe whether it call itself my home, my fatherland or my church; and I will try to express myself in some mode of life or art as freely- silence, exile, and cunning...*

Joyce; *A discussion with my mother...Then she said I would come back to faith because I had a restless mind...I cannot repent. Told her so and asked for six-pence. Got threepence...*

Mother is putting my new second hand clothes in order. She prays now she says, that I may learn in my own life and away from home and friends what the heart is and what it feels. Amen. So be it. Welcome! O life! I go to encounter for the millionth time the reality of experience and so to forge in the smithy of my soul the uncreated conscience of my race...Old father, old artificer, stand me now and ever in good stead[60].

---

[60] . *Portrait of the Artist as a Young Man,* Jonathan Cape 1952. pp. 243-257

John Francis Byrne [Cranley] felt that James had been heartless to his mother and told him so. He was even angrier when James sought to use religion to defend himself, while at the same time proclaiming his liberty from religion. Byrne adds that James was never at ease with older people[61].

When the controversy over Synge's *Playboy of the Western World* occurred in Dublin, James traumatized Stanislaus by supporting those Nationalists who rioted in the Abbey Theatre against the play as a travesty against Irish people. " *I read of a riot in a Dublin theatre, a clerk named Patrick Colm up at the Police Courts for disorderly conduct in the Abbey Theatre at a performance of Synge's play 'Playboy of the Western World' reviews in Sinn Fein have been hostile. I believe Column and the Irish Theatre will beat Yeats, Lady Gregory and Miss Horniman which will please me greatly as Yeats cannot hawk his theatre over to London. Senor Bulfin has a letter in Sinn Fein ridiculing a Union Jack Regatta in Galway*" [1/2/07] James was sorry he was not in Dublin for the occasion.

He had ceased to write and continued his spendthrift ways drinking and pauperising Nora and Georgio and pestering Stanislaus for money. He wrote Stan on 6 September 1906, *"I want money. I have written quite enough and before I do any more in that line, I must see some reason why – I am not a literary Jesus Christ".*

He told Stan on 11 /2/07 from Rome "Yeats is a tiresome idiot: he is quite out of touch with the Irish people, to which he appeals as the author of Countess Kathleen. Synge is better; at least he can set them by the ears...as I told you I think the Abbey Theatre is ruined. It is supported by the stalls that is to say, Stephen Gwynn, Lord X, Lady Gregory etc who are dying to relieve the monotony of Dublin life".

---

[61]. Byrne JF. . pp.86-7

One of James' main achievements in Rome was to assemble his thoughts on the architecture of what was to be the "*lynchpin*' of his writing, and the final story in *Dubliners, The Dead*. In this he saw the positive elements in Dublin life and began to defend his country when it came under attack. Like many more before and after him, he discovered the positive elements of his heritage in exile. He wrote of *Dubliners* without *The Dead:*

Sometimes thinking of Ireland it seems to me that I have been unnecessarily harsh. I have reproduced [in Dubliners at least] none of the attraction of the city for I have never felt at ease in any city since I left it except in Paris. I have not reproduced its ingenuous insularity and its hospitality. The latter 'virtue' so far as I can see does not exist elsewhere in Europe. I have not been unduly kind just to its beauty; for it is more beautiful naturally in my opinion than what I have seen of England, Switzerland, France, Austria or Italy.

He rectified this when he added "*The Dead*" to the collection of stories that make up "*Dubliners*". Like many people before him he came to recognise the positive elements of his heritage, after leave-taking it. He became a Dubliner, an Irishman, in Rome and in Trieste. He wrote '*The Dead*' in 1906-7 after he returned to Trieste. Like all his other stories it is significantly autobiographical. In it he makes amends to Dublin and Ireland allowing some of their warmth to enter. As Ellmann writes, "*In its lyrical, melancholy acceptance of all that life and death offer, 'The Dead' is a lynchpin in Joyce's work*"[62]. In the last scene as Gabriel discovers that his wife Gretta has had a life and a lover in Galway before meeting him and that it remains vividly in her psyche, we can see all too clearly that Joyce is writing about

---

[62] .Ellmann Richard, *James Joyce*, Oxford 1983. P. 252.

himself and Nora and the distance that comes between them, despite his own desperate love and need for Nora's love. As Hugh Kenner writes, *"For Joyce was in so many ways nearly Stephen as he was nearly Mr. Duffy in 'A Painful Case' and nearly Gabriel Conroy in 'The Dead' and nearly Bloom in 'Ulysses' "*[63]

On 25 /9/'06 he wrote Stan, " *On way home from The Forum being very tired I went into a Dominican Church where I found a comfortable straw chair. I watched two nuns at confession...knelt down beside me. Then Vespers began. Then there was the rosary. Then there was a sermon. The gentleman who delivered it addressed most of his remarks to me – God knows why. I suppose I looked pious. I didn't wait for Benediction... ".* On 10/1/07 he wrote Stan, *"They are celebrating this week in Sylvester's Church the union of the rites. Every morning a different rite. I should love to go. But I may as well be in Cabra for all I see of anything Coptic, Greek, Chaldean etc".*

In need of a change he resigned his post in the bank in Rome writing Stan on 16/2/07 " *I gave notice here on Thursday. If I will be permitted I will resume teaching at the school. Artifioni promised me I could go back when I liked...I have come to the conclusion that it is about time I made up my mind whether I am a writer or a patient Cousins "*[64]. He had explored the prospect of work in other cities but decided to return to Trieste. Stanislaus was apoplectic to hear this and tried to dissuade James saying that Artifoni had told him that there was no job for his brother at the Berlitz. In February came the rejection by John Long of *Dubliners* and the news that the disaffected Nora was pregnant. After being assaulted and robbed during one of his drunken sessions in Rome he took the train to Trieste.

---

[63] . Kenner Hugh, *the Pound Era,* Faber 1972, p. 273.

[64] . This is a reference to James Cousins in whose house in Sandymount Dublin he had stayed for a short period.

The very frustrated and exasperated Stanislaus met them at the station. Neither brother had any money. Francini took the family in for a few days. Artifoni did not need another teacher but feared James might poach students from him, especially those well-off students whom Joyce had already taught and who regarded him highly. So he gave James six hours a week teaching. One of those students was Roberto Prezioso, acting editor of *Il Piccolo della Serra* and political editor of *Il Piccolo*, who due to James' poor circumstances and his own anti-Imperialism, decided that he would commission some articles, in Italian, from James on the negative experiences of Ireland living under Empire. He wrote three articles after which he told Stanislaus that, "*I may not be the Jesus Christ I once fondly imagined myself, but I think I must have a talent for journalism*".

Joyce was very glad to be back in Trieste. While living there he occasionally attended the Jewish synagogue. One thousand Jews had come to Trieste in 1891 from Corfu and formed part of the community despite attempts to encourage them to move on. James was sympathetic to them as is clear from *Ulysses* where he writes, "*Jews, whom Christians tax with avarice, are of all races the most given to intermarriage. Accusations are made in anger. The Christian laws which built up the hoards of the Jews bound their affections too with hoops of steel*". James was also conscious that just as Ireland is the country in which Irishmen are to be found, though there were more Irishmen outside of Ireland than in it, Palestine would so become for Jews. He would later have Leopold Bloom say, "I *stand for reform of municipal morals and the plain ten commandments. New world for old. Union of all, jew, moslem and gentile. Three acres and a cow for all children of nature. Saloon motor hearses. Compulsory labour for all. All parks open to the public day and night*"[65].

In Paris Joyce would again identify Jews as being an oppressed people, *'Not theirs; these clothes, this speech, these gestures', rather cast offs from overlords, just like the Irish and looking for a scapegoat who will combine all the despised elements in himself; Leopold Bloom.* Joyce illustrates this as a neo-colonial act in the scene in Sandycove Tower where he the Irishman pays his rent while Haines/Kinch the Englishman goes free under the despised Irish landlord, Buck Mulligan. Terence Killeen identifies one Italo Svevo a friend of James' from Trieste as exhibiting elements of Bloom's character, diffidence, some, cynicism, gentleness, reasonableness, breadth of sympathies[66]

---

[65] . *Ulysses.* 15.1685.93.

[66] . Killeen Terence Irish Times book review of *'James Joyce and Italo Svevo; the Story of a Friendship* by Stanley Price, Somerville Press 2016. 12 Nov 2016.

CHAPTER 4.

IRISH NATIONALIST?

Stanislaus Joyce described Arthur Griffith *as "a rather insignificant-looking man, with none of Parnell's glamour and advised James to support the parliamentarism of Tom Kettle".* James rejected this stating that the Irish Parliamentary Party (IPP) had gone bankrupt. James supported the Sinn Fein view that the Irish were understandably disloyal to the British monarch because they were the victims of misrule. At the same time he did not believe that the oppressed were free of guilt or that rule by one's own would of necessity be easier. However he did move some way from his earlier harsh admonitions in his review of Willie Rooney's poems coming from *'Headquarters'*. In the series of articles for Prezioso's paper by Joyce on the parallel of Ireland under British rule during 1907, James outlined some parallels with Trieste and Austria. At a later lecture delivered at the Universitá Popolare he did the same. For both exercises he agreed a fee of 25 crowns. For the lecture he borrowed a suit from Artifoni and an overcoat from Stanislaus. A large crowd assembled in the Sala della Borsa. Nora who did not have suitable clothes for the occasion went to the cinema with Georgio[67]. It is also clear that many of his 'more mature' reflections on Irish history reflect his close reading of the *United Irishman* and the natural adherence to the land of his birth, of an exile or emigrant. He stated candidly:

---

[67] .McCourt p. 117.

"If a victorious country terrorises over another, it cannot reasonably take it amiss if the latter responds. Men are made that way and no-one, unless he is deluded by self-interest or cunning, can still believe that a colonizing country is driven by purely Christian motives when it takes over foreign shores - - if the Irish have not been able to do what their American brothers did, this does not mean that they will never do so - - a moral separation already exists between the two countries".

Joyce realised that it might be naïve to be indignant with England over her misdeeds in Ireland. He said that such was the *modus vivendi* of colonisers all over the world, including that of Belgium in the Congo Free State. They despoiled the country economically, divided the people and persecuted their religion. Kevin Barry writes of the contrast between this Trieste material and Joyce's earlier contributions to the *Daily Express*. He says that almost all of Joyce's writing material is drawn from Arthur Griffith's own writings in the *United Irishman* and its successor *Sinn Fein*[68]. The practicality of Griffith's emphasis on trade and consuls abroad, replacing Irish Members of Parliament at Westminster, appealed to him. It appears that Joyce sent his articles to Griffith who published them anonymously. On 19 January 1907 an article on theatre carried the by-line '*J.P. Ruhart*', one of Griffith's own pen names. The first report on '*An Irish Consular Service Abroad*' which Joyce liked, appeared on 19 May 1906.

The front pages of Griffith's *Sinn Fein* through 1906-1909 invariably contained the same lay-out, with three main sections given to Branch Reports on *The National Council, Gaelic League and the Gaelic Athletic Association.* Other regular features in the paper were:

---

[68] . Barry Kevin, ed. *James Joyce Occasional Writings,* Oxford University Press, 2008

Industrial Movement, Ireland & Foreign Trade, Dublin Corporation, The International Exhibition, Over the Frontier, Rambles in Eirinn, The Irish Bogs. Regular advertisements, of which there were many, included: *Kennedys Bread, Hopkins & Hopkins Jewellers, JM Collins Tailors, Madigan Bros., MH Gill & Son, Saffron Clothing, Keogh Donnelly Ltd. Ham & Bacon, Dixons' Dublin Soaps, Cathal McGarvey Entertainments.* Rooney's *Poems & Ballads* was still being advertised during these years.

John O'Leary

An article titled *Il Fenianismo* was published to mark the centenary of the death of John O'Leary on St Patrick's Day, and built around O'Leary's long separatist career[69]. Joyce declared his faith in Sinn Féin saying that the new Fenians have regrouped in a party called Sinn Féin. They aimed to make Ireland a bilingual republic and to this end, they have established a direct ferry link between Ireland and France. They boycott English goods and refuse to become soldiers or swear an oath of allegiance to the British crown. They endeavour to develop the industry of the whole country and rather than pay one and a quarter millions each year to maintain the eighty deputies in the English Parliament, they want to set up a consular service in the major

---

[69] . On the anniversary of the centenary of John O'Leary's death in March 2007 no commemoration was planned. I gave notice through the letters page of the *Irish Times* that there would be a poetry recital at his grave in Glasnevin Cemetery. A small group were present as I recited some of WB Yeats' commemorative verses.

world ports with the aim of marketing industrial produce, without the intrusion of England. From many points of view this latest form of Fenianism is the most formidable. Its influence has certainly once again remoulded the character of the Irish.

Joyce sent a copy of this article to Eugene Sheehy, whom he had not met for several years. John O'Leary had once presided at one of their University College Debates in Dublin. Sheehy knew that before Joyce had left Dublin he was adept at Italian[70].

Joyce predicted correctly that the British Conservatives would conspire to incite Ulster Unionists to rebel against any settlement with the leadership in Dublin. Declan Kiberd writes, *"This was one of the most accurate predictions of partition"*[71]. Ireland remained poor because English laws were designed systematically to ruin the country's industries. As Griffith knew better than most in later years and as Joyce wrote, the future Irish Government will have to cover a deficit ably created by the British Treasury. Joyce deemed Griffith's *United Irishman* the only paper of any merit in Ireland. He wrote to Stanislaus of Griffith, *"so far as my knowledge of Irish affairs goes, he was the first person in Ireland to revive the separatist idea on modern lines nine years ago. He wants the creation of an Irish consular service abroad and of an Irish bank at home"*.

Joyce thought Griffith unassuming and sensible and supported his call for an economic boycott of Britain, writing to Stanislaus on 24 April 1907, that *'The Sinn Fein policy comes to fighting England with the knife and fork...the highest form of political warfare I have heard of"*. The policy of Sinn Fein, if rigorously followed, would bring about political and economic independence at home, just as Joyce abroad,

---

[70] . Sheehy Richard *May it Please the Court My Lord* p. 27-28.
[71] . Kiberd Declan *Inventing Ireland* p. 335.

would achieve the necessary artistic independence for his countrymen to import. He thought that his own spiritual task might have to wait upon Griffith's economic one, as people then haven't the time or stomach to think. Griffith sought political and economic independence while James sought artistic and spiritual independence for his countrymen to import. Despite his nationalist fervour Joyce retained his belief that the Irish had a penchant for betraying their leaders, though they also had a habit of giving them great funerals. He was no doubt putting himself on that list though ironically that outcome might also have been the fate of Griffith himself.

Gogarty and Joyce had a very strained relationship which continued with both determined to do down the other. Gogarty wrote in later life, *"Joyce was an unlovable and lonely man; but he willed his life. He was an artist deliberately and naturally and for this he sacrificed everything, even his humanity. He imagined that an artist was someone detached from humanity - an observer, and an inhuman one at that. This dehumanization and a decent lack of reticence and a persecution complex roused in him an indignation which enabled him to scrawl - as it were on the dead walls of the city – the most indecent graffito of decadence ever written: his Ulysses".*

TWO LETTERS FROM FATHER

James received two unexpected letters from his father in early 1907. They both illustrate common characteristics between father and son.

9 Millmount Tce Drive Drumcondra   21 March 1907

Dear Jim, ...I am forced to the conclusion that I have entirely faded out of your memory and of Stan's. Well I am now so accustomed to all sorts of unnatural treatment since your mother died, both from you and those here...

7 Whitworth road Drumcondra 16 May 1907

Dear Jim,   You will dare say be surprised at receiving this letter...I fear the end is coming in more respects than one...I feel certain I have seen my last Xmas...my last shilling went on a Sunday dinner..."

Lucia was born in the summer of 1907 to the disappointment of both parents as they had been hoping for a boy[72]. James' attempts to get work from Italian newspapers as an Irish correspondent failed and he had to survive on his *'meagre part-time salary'* from the Berlitz School.

In late September 1907 when Grant Richards responded to James saying that he would not publish *Dubliners*. James, through the English consul, consulted a lawyer about this breach of contract. Despite further contacts including legal letters and James' capitulation on dropping two whole stories and modifying others, Grant Richards still refused to alter his decision not to publish. James was very angry and frustrated. Stanislaus, as always, tried to bolster him to continue writing. James retorted by again comparing himself to Jesus saying that he was not a literary Jesus Christ willing to sacrifice himself for the good of others; he wanted to see some results first. In November James offered the book to John Long.

James then directed his attention to attempting to have his poetry collection published, though realising that he would not earn any money from that. Arthur Symonds, a British poet, critic and magazine editor recommended them to Elkin Mathews a British publisher and bookseller, who responded, *"I am very much obliged to you for*

---

[72] . McCourt p. 123.

drawing my attention to Mr. Joyce's work and feel sure from what you tell me of its quality that it will be a great acquisition to my Vigo series. So will you please put me into communication with Mr. Joyce or arrange with him for me to see his MSS"[73]. James consulted Stanislaus on their presentation. Stanislaus preferred the original title of 'Chamber Music'. James affected a disinterest in his poetry, saying that he was not a poet but that they were a part of his youth and he wished to have them out of the way. It was published by Elkin Mathews in April 1907 priced at 1/6. The print run was 509 copies consisting of thirty-four love poems. It was fairly well reviewed but it made no money for him as royalties only kicked in after a certain amount of sales which it struggled for several years to achieve. Tom Kettle reviewed it and echoed some of Joyce's later feeling about *'Dubliners'* without *'The Dead'*. Kettle wrote: *Those who remember University College life of some years back will have many memories of Mr. Joyce; wilful, fastidious, a lover of elfish paradoxes...here is no trace of the folklore, folk dialect, or even the national feeling that have coloured the work of practically every writer in contemporary Ireland...there is an economic and there is a spiritual exile. It is clear, delicate, distinguished playing*"[74]. Arthur Symonds reviewed it saying, *..There is a rare kind of poetry to be made out of the kind or unkind insinuations of lovers...There is no substance at all in these songs, which hardly hint at a story; but they are like a whispering clavichord that someone plays in the evening, when it is getting dark....How unlikely it seems, does it not, that any new thing should come suddenly into the world and be beautiful*[75].

---

[73] . Gorman p. 174.
[74] . Freeman's Journal 1 June 1907.
[75] Gorman. p. 193.

James was later pleased to have some of the poems set to music by G. Molyneux Palmer in 1909.

One poem reads:

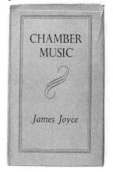

Lean out of the window,

Golden hair,
I hear you singing
A merry air.

My book is closed;
I read no more,
Watching the fire dance
On the floor.

I have left my books;
I have left my room;
For I heard you singing
Through the gloom.

Singing and singing
A merry air.
Lean out of the window
Golden hair.

During that turbulent summer of 1907 James became ill. The Berlitz School had been taken over by two employees. When James discovered that his debts to the school were being transferred to the new owners he resigned '*in a fury*' to become an independent teacher of English in Trieste[76]. He completed T*he Dead* on 20 September and began a rewrite of Stephen Hero. Despite his and his family's on-going impecunious and impoverished state and his continued drunken

---

[76] . McCourt p. 127.

behaviour, he was able to get free tickets from Francini of *Piccolo della Sera* for the theatre, which he attended regularly. He translated JM Synge's R*iders to the Sea* into Italian but was refused permission by Synge's heirs to stage it[77]. The only thing that stopped his drinking temporarily was when it affected his eye sight and Nora's threat to have the children baptised.

Elkin Mathews who published *Chamber Music* turned down James' *Dubliners,* but sent it to Joseph Hone of Maunsel publishers in Dublin. Hutchinson of London refused it without sight; Alston Rivers turned it down in Feb 1908 and Edward Arnold in July. Joseph Hone asked officially to see the manuscript in Feb 1908 but Joyce still wanted it published in London. He did not send it to Maunsel until April 1909.

James had still not become officially reconciled to his father since his elopement. To make amends he talked about sending Georgio to Dublin with Stanislaus for the summer of 1909. He ran the idea past his sister Margaret who was in charge of running the family home then at 44 Fontenoy St. Dublin. He ended the letter, *"Hoping this will find you as it leaves me at present, thank God, I am dear sister, your Most Affectionate Brother Jim".* In July 1909 James got a large advance from one of his students and decided that he and Georgio would travel to Dublin. All the while the great work of *Ulysses* was burgeoning in his brain.

---

[77] . Ellmann Richard p. 267.

Chapter   5.

TWO TRIPS TO IRELAND IN 1909

James Connolly said that his two greatest mistakes were first to go to America and secondly to return to Ireland. Joyce saw himself as the prodigal son. He wrote in his play *Exiles*, *"It is dangerous to leave one's country, but still more dangerous to go back to it, for then your fellow-countrymen, if they can, will drive a knife into your heart"*. Jim wrote Nora on 4 August from the family home on 44 Fontenoy St., *"We arrived safely here tonight. All are delighted with Georgio, especially Pappie"*. All the while during his visit back in Ireland James was, as always, storing up material for his writings. He faced many varied challenges in returning to Dublin. His family were naturally excited by seeing him again, this time with his son. He and Georgio were welcomed by the family with his father quickly making peace with his errant son. Dublin being a small place meant that James could have met most of his old acquaintances quite quickly, if he had chosen to do so. But he ignored some and adopted a cool formal demeanour to most, while entirely rejecting Oliver Gogarty's attempts to be friendly. He wrote to Stan on 4 August, *"Gogarty met me on Merrion Square, so I passed. He ran after me and took my arm and made a long speech. I said 'you have your life. Leave me to mine".*

James needed to bolster his need to continue to play the role of the rejected one, the betrayed, the Parnell, the Jesus Christ. One of his greatest challenges or opportunities to play this role came from an old friend Vincent Cosgrave, who had been acquainted with Nora in Dublin prior to James meeting her[78]. Cosgrave intimated that Nora had gone *out'* with him even while she was seeing James in Dublin. This apparent faithlessness undermined one of the bulwarks of James' operational capacity. He was devastated and in a state of utter desperation. He planned to leave Dublin immediately. He wrote two letters of great and intimate detail to Nora demanding to know what exactly had happened between herself and Cosgrave. The first letter ended with:

"O, Nora, I am unhappy. I am crying for my poor unhappy love. Write to me, Nora"; the second, " "If I could forget my books and my children and forget that the girl I loved was false to me and remember her only as I saw her with the eyes of my boyish love I would go out of life content. How old and miserable I feel". He asked her, *"Is Georgio my son. O Nora I have been a fool".*

7 Eccles St.   Gogarty

The pain was so great that James could not contain it within himself. He went to visit another college friend John Francis Byrne in 7 Eccles

[78]. Maddox Breda *Nora A Biography of Nora Joyce*, Hamish Hamilton1988. P. 129.

St. and poured out the whole story. Byrne recalled, "*I had always known that Joyce was highly emotional but I had never before this afternoon seen anything to approach the frightening condition that convulsed him. He wept and groaned and gesticulated in futile impotence as he sobbed out to me that the thing had occurred. Never in my life have I seen a human being more shattered...*"[79]. Byrne had listened carefully to his guest and was able deduce that Cosgrave's story was a lie and part of a conspiracy, possibly with Gogarty, to destroy Joyce. This was the perfect antidote to heal James' nightmare as it fitted in perfectly with his long-held experience of Gogarty. Joyce stayed the night with Byrne and went off happily in the morning. He soon began to feel very guilty of believing such a story about Nora. When she did not reply to his letters he wrote after a fortnight telling her of what Byrne had said and asking for forgiveness. Yet he asked for "*a word of denial*", promising that in future he would be worthy of her love. He wrote "*No man, I believe, can ever be worthy of a woman's love*". In a very real way Joyce, especially in his sexually explicit letters to her, expected Nora to act as a virgin and a whore and began to resent having to share her with their two children[80]. He was always wary of her threats to leave him.

Meanwhile in Trieste Nora was feeling devastated. She did not reply immediately to James' two letters but showed them to Stanislaus who was very supportive. He was able to corroborate the lie told by Cosgrave through a contemporary incident when the latter had confided in him his failure to '*go out*' with Nora. She wrote to James movingly acknowledging his love for her and admitting that he possibly should break with her, yet retaining her dignity and ignoring his demand for a denial. Instead she told him that she was reading the

[79] . Byrne JF, *Silent Years* p. 156.
[80] . Maddox Breda *Nora A Biography of Nora Joyce*, Hamish Hamilton1988. p. 132-3.

poems in *Chamber Music*. He replied that though the poems were not written about her *"there was something in you higher than anything I had put into them"*. He wrote two letters to Nora;

21 August 44 Fontenoy St

My Dear little Nora,

I think you are in love with me, are you not…Have I been cruel to You?

4 Bowling Green Galway 26 August

Nora,

How sick, sick sick I am of Dublin! It is the city of failure, of rancour and of unhappiness. I long to be out of it".

In the totally self-centred righteous fashion of tragic artists James began to play the victim with Nora, demanding that she make amends so that he could love her all the more. He wrote *"your love for me must be fierce and violent to make me forget utterly"*. She met his wishes by writing the erotic letter demanded[81].

James and Georgio spent a weekend in Galway meeting Nora's relations, the Healys and the Barnacles. They were warmly responded to. James listened to Nora's mother talk and sing. His passion and love for Nora during that weekend was immense as he wrote to her that one day they might both return to her home town. On 4 August James met Frank Skeffington and Hanna Sheehy on the street. He wrote to Stanislaus, *"Kettle marries Mary Sheehy on 8 September…Kathleen marries Cruise O'Brien"*. James later attended

---

[81] . Maddox Breda *Nora A Biography of Nora Joyce*, Hamish Hamilton1988. P. 131.

a reception in the Gresham Hotel in connection with his friend Tom Kettles' marriage to Mary Sheehy in September[82]. There he received high praise among his contemporaries as the coming Irish writer. James then saw his love for Nora as akin to the patriot's love for his country or a believer's love for God who would subsume his body and soul.

As usual James borrowed money from many sources while in Dublin. These included George Roberts who gave him an advance on royalties for *Dubliners*. Margaret Joyce left home during James' visit to become a Sister of Mercy in New Zealand. His sister Eva returned to Trieste with him. Stanislaus, who had borne all the expenses involved in the visit to Dublin, expected to hear much news of Dublin from James. But he was rudely rebuffed as James and Nora acted like reconciled lovers on his return with time only for her.

THE *VOLTA*

It was from his sister Eva Joyce, who liked the new experience of going to the cinema in Trieste, that James got the idea of starting a cinema in Dublin, which had none. He persuaded some local businessmen that an opportunity for opening cinemas existed in Ireland and he could provide the local knowledge required. Within a month of returning from Dublin he embarked again on the return journey. He explored the technicalities involved and invited the investors to come to Dublin, where he booked them into Finn's Hotel. These were four Italians: Antonio Machnich, an upholsterer, and Giovanni Rebez, a leather merchant, Giusppe Caris, a draper, Francesco Novak, the owner of a bicycle shop. They owned two picture houses in Trieste and one in Bucharest. They had been suitably impressed by Joyce and appointed him their Irish agent at

---

[82] . Callanan Frank *The Myth of Tom Kettle* Irish Times 10 May 2016. . Kathleen Sheehy did not marry Frank Skeffington until 7 October 1911.

10% of all monies made from the new Irish operation and an allowance of 10 Austrian crowns (about eight shillings) a day. Machnich and Rebez visited Dublin, Belfast and Cork[83]. In Belfast on 27 November Joyce also went in search of Belfast linen and bought some sheets. He rounded off that Saturday with the conviviality of WB Reynolds music critic of the Belfast Evening Telegraph. Reynolds was the first Rathcol music columnist of the Telegraph. He was also to set some of Joyce's lyrics to music, including '*She Weeps over Rahoon*'[84]

The Investors then brought two colleagues to Dublin to manage the cinema business. James was involved in all the detailed preparations interviewing local staff, buying seating, securing advertisements. Eventually on 20 December 1909 the Volta Cinema on Mary St

Dublin opened. The Evening Telegraph wrote, "Yesterday *at 45 Mary St a most interesting cinematograph exhibition was opened before a large number of invited guests. The hall in which the display takes place is most admirably equipped for the purpose, and has been admirably laid out. Indeed, no expense would appear to have been spared in making the entertainment one deserving of the patronage of the public….An excellent little string*

[83] . Price Stanley. p. 96.
[84] . *Belfast Telegraph* 27/11/1909.

orchestra played charmingly during the afternoon. Mr. James Joyce, who is in charge of the exhibition, has worked apparently indefatigably in its production and deserves to be congratulated on the success of the inaugural exhibition"[85]. The opening night featured an eclectic program, with the comedy *Devilled Crab*, the mystery *Bewitched Castle, La Pourponièrre, The First Paris Orphanage*, and *The Tragedy of Beatrice Cency*. The cinema mainly showed films from Europe and Italy, which were largely ignored by Dubliners at the time. After seven months, Joyce became disillusioned with the venture and withdrew his involvement and the cinema was sold at a loss to the *British Provincial Cinema Company*. The cinema stayed open until 1919.

James was so busy during these few months that apart from his own family he saw little of his usual acquaintances, though he did see George Roberts who assured him that the galley proofs for *Dubliners* were being prepared.

As on his last absence from Nora he missed her terribly, but at first could not resist challenging her love for him, because she did not on every occasion give him her undivided attention. He thought because he believed he was engaged on important literary work that nothing else mattered, not even his bad behaviour to her and everyone else. He did not consider who was to fund the household while he was away despite a court writ being served for payment of rent. Nora chided him and he responded with sexually explicit letters to which Nora joined in egging him on to pornographic and masochistic practices which they had experimented with. As Brenda Maddox writes, *"The wonder is not that James Joyce could do it but that Nora Barnacle, schooled only at the Convent of Mercy, confidently matched him and, by his own judgement, sometimes bettered him"*[86]. He was her man and she intended to do what it took to hold on to him. He might be superior to her in some ways but she was a match for him in life. He acted like a mischievous child with her, whose whims and exaggerations had to be chastised and understood and forgiven, so

---

[85]. The Evening Telegraph 20/12/1909.
[86]. Maddox Brenda p. 141.

that he could restate his love for his queen. The fact that he was a writer made little impression on her as she remained thoroughly impassive about it even as his reputation grew over the succeeding years. She took little or no interest in what he was creating. He found this difficult to understand but had to accept the reality from his darling wife. His visit to Finn's Hotel and to her room evoked tears, a sacred fire burning in his soul on the altar. He could have *"knelt and prayed there as the three kings from the east knelt and prayed before the manger in which Jesus lay…I had brought my errors and follies and sins and wonderings and longing to lay them at the little bed in which a young girl I had dreamed of me"*.

James left Dublin on 2 January 1910 taking his sister Eileen with him despite Stanislaus' objections. His eyes were giving him great trouble and it was several weeks before he was able to resume his teaching. The Joyce sisters went to Mass regularly. James too went on occasion though emphasising he went there for cultural performance reasons. Nora did not attend. The sisters were scandalised to discover that James and Nora were not married. She was open to a ceremony but he was not. The presence of the sisters proved beneficial to Nora who was again able to converse in her natural language and find companionship. The usual state of penury continued as relations between the brothers further deteriorated. Eva did not remain in Trieste but returned home in July of 1911.

Chapter 6.

TRYING TO PUBLISH DUBLINERS

James was again sorely disappointed early in 1911 over *Dubliners*. He wrote to Roberts on 3 January asking, *Is that book to be published as you write, on 20 January definitely?* On 22 January he wrote to Stan, *Dubliners announced for publication for the third time yesterday 20 January, is again postponed sine die and without a word of explanation. I know the name and tradition of my country too well to be surprised at receiving three scrawled lines in return for five years of constant service to my art...Since they drove me out of that hospitable bog six years ago...* In February he wrote Stan, *I have no money whatsoever. Four new pupils next week. Kindly come here unless we are to starve.*

The main hope James had of making any money was through the publication of *'Dubliners'*. But George Roberts continued to prevaricate. He then began to demand the omission of insulting references to King Edward VII from the story, *Ivy Day at the Committee*. Edward VII was a well-known rake. James consulted a Dublin solicitor who advised him to accede to Robert's demand as any court action would most likely fail. Six months later James wrote to Roberts, *"If no reply is sent me to this letter I shall consider that you have no intention of publishing the book and shall communicate the whole matter of the dispute in a circular letter to the Irish press and at the same time take legal action against you through my solicitor in Dublin for breach of contract"*. James was only bluffing in part; as he took what he hoped might be decisive action.

CONSULTING KING GEORGE V

George v   Edward VII

James then undertook another stratagem by writing directly to the son of Edward VII who had succeeded his father, George V. He included the 'offending' passage on Edward VII and asked George V to adjudicate on whether it was insulting to his late father. Unlike the tale about the student in Clongowes successfully approaching the Rector for adjudication, George V did not respond. His private secretary did reply saying why the King could not respond, *"It is inconsistent with the rules…………."* But the letter to the King was only part of his plan. He then sent his correspondence to the King to various newspapers giving his side of the story on the history of his endeavours to have *"Dubliners"* published. He calculated that if a newspaper did publish his material in full, this would demonstrate to publishers that there was nothing to worry about in the passage to which Roberts objected. He sent the letter to several newspapers. The only editor who published it in full was Arthur Griffith in his *"Sinn Fein"*. The *Northern Whig* ran an edited version. Griffith who had defended the student Joyce against censorship so many years earlier, had clearly forgiven Joyce's critical review of Willie Rooney's poems. Griffith, so lacking in symptoms of self-importance, was again happy to support him as an Irish artist involved in important literary creation abroad. Griffith was astute enough to know what Joyce was about and to play his part in the plan. James was careful enough to send copies of Griffith's paper directly to George Roberts and Grant Richards.

HISTORY OF REJECTIONS BY PUBLISHERS

The letter read:

"Dubliners"

To The Editor of Sinn Fein,

Sir,

May I ask you to publish this letter which throws some light on the present conditions of authorship in England and Ireland?

Nearly six years ago Mr. Grant Richards, publisher, of London, signed a contract with me for the publication of a book of stories written by me entitled "Dubliners". Some ten months later he wrote asking me to omit one of the stories and passages in others which, as he said, his printer refused to set up. I declined to do either and a correspondence between Mr. Grant Richards and myself ensued which lasted more than three months. I went to an international jurist in Rome (where I lived then) and was advised to omit. I declined to do so and the manuscript was returned to me, the publisher refusing to publish, notwithstanding his pledged printed word, the contract remaining in my possession.

Six months afterwards a Mr. Hone wrote to me from Marseilles to ask me to submit the manuscript to Messrs Maunsel publisher of Dublin. I did so; and after about a year, in July 1909, Messrs Maunsel's signed a contract with me for the publication of the book on or before 1st September, 1910. In December, 1909, Messrs Maunsel's manager begged me to alter a passage in one of the stories, " Ivy Day in the Committee Room", wherein some reference was made to Edward VII. I agreed to do so, much against my will, and altered one or two phrases. Messrs Maunsel continuously postponed the date of publication and in the end wrote, asking me to omit the passage or to change it radically. I declined to do either, pointing out that Mr. Grant Richards of London had raised no objection to the passage when Edward VII was alive, and that I could not see why an Irish publisher should raise an objection to it when Edward VII had passed into history. I suggested arbitration, or a deletion of the passage, with a prefatory note of explanation by me, but Messrs Maunsel would agree to neither. As Mr. Hone (who had written to me in the first instance) disclaimed any responsibility in the matter, and any connection with the firm, I took the opinion of a solicitor in Dublin, who advised me to omit the passage, informing me that as I had no domicile in the United Kingdom I could not sue Messrs Maunsel for breach of contract unless I paid £100 into court, and sued them. I should have no chance of getting a verdict in my favour from a Dublin jury if the passage in dispute could be taken as offensive in any way to the late King.

I wrote to the present King, King George V[87], enclosing a printed proof of the story, with the passage therein marked, and begging him

---

[87] . George's Hall in Dublin Castle was built for the July 1911 visit to Dublin of George V. He was the last reigning British monarch to visit Dublin until the recent visit of Elizabeth II.

to inform me whether in his view the passage (certain allusions made by a person of the story in the idiom of his social class) should be held from publication as offensive to the memory of his father. His Majesty's private secretary sent me this reply:-

Buckingham Palace

11th August 1911

The private secretary is commanded to acknowledge the receipt of Mr. James Joyce's letter of the 1st instance and to inform him that it is inconsistent with the rule for His Majesty to express his opinion in such cases. The enclosures are returned herewith".

HERE IS THE PASSAGE IN DISPUTE:

"But look here, John said Mr. O'Connor. 'Why should we welcome the King of England? Didn't Parnell himself...'

'Parnell' said Mr. Henchy 'is dead. Now, here's the way I look at it. Here's this chap come to the throne after his old mother keeping him out of it till the man was grey. He's a man of the world, and he means well by us. He's a jolly, fine decent fellow, if you ask me, and no damn nonsense about him. He just says to himself: "The old one never went to see these wild Irish. By Christ, I'll go myself and see what they're like." And are we going to insult the man when he comes over here on a friendly visit? Eh? Isn't that right Crofton?'

Mr. Crofton nodded his head.

'But after all now' said Mr. Lyons argumentatively, 'King Edward's life, you know, is not eh very...'

'Let bygones be bygones' said Mr. Henchy, 'I admire the man personally. He's just an ordinary knockabout like you and me. He's fond of his glass of grog and he's a bit of a rake, perhaps, and he's a

good sportsman. Damn it, can't we Irish play fair?"

I wrote this book seven years ago and hold two contracts for its publication. I am not even allowed to explain my case in a prefatory note; wherefore, as I cannot see in any quarter a chance that my rights will be protected, I hereby give Messrs. Maunsel publicly, permission to publish this story with what changes or deletions they may please to make and shall hope that what they may publish, may resemble that to the writing of which I gave thought and time. Their attitude as an Irish publishing firm may be judged by Irish public opinion. I, as a writer, protest against the systems (legal, social and ceremonious) which have brought me to this pass. Thanking you for your courtesy.

I am, Sir, Your obedient servant. James Joyce 17 August 1911[88].

Unfortunately despite James' effort the rouse had no effect on George Roberts who ignored it entirely. Meantime James decided that he would try to get a job teaching English in an Italian public school. The formalities were complex yet he applied himself assiduously until Italian bureaucracy defeated him.

One of the very many examples where it is evident that so much of Joyce's writings are based on real even and real people can be seen in the poignant story of '*Araby*' in *Dubliners*. WG Fallon recalls meeting Joyce on the very evening that he went to this bazaar to buy the present he had marked out for his girlfriend. Fallon had just got off the train at Lansdowne Road on a Saturday night. When they reached the bazaar it was just ending. Fallon saw that Joyce was disheartened over something[89]. This practice of Joyce naturally made publishers wary of people taking libel cases against them.

---

[88] . *United Irishman* 17 /11/1911
[89] . O'Connor Ulick Ed. Fallon WG. In *the Joyce we Knew*. P. 48.

Chapter 7.

FINAL TRAUMATIC VISIT TO IRELAND 1912

Nora got the opportunity to visit Galway in the summer of 1912 with
the younger children, when her uncle Michael Healy sent her the
money for a ticket. James approved of the trip on the basis that she
would seek to meet George Roberts and try to convince him to
publish "*Dubliners*". He would not agree to Nora's wish to wear a
ring on her wedding finger for the trip. Her arrival with Lucia at
Westland Row station was met by a large number of Dublin Joyces
including John, who had become a frequent correspondent with her,
since his reconciliation with James in 1909. John invited her to dinner
in Finn's hotel and they had a day's outing to Howth. Her visit to
George Roberts, accompanied by John and Charley Joyce was
ineffectual. Then she travelled to Galway. Meantime James was going
through his usual panic without Nora, especially when she did not
write to him immediately on arrival in Dublin. Within a few days he
had decided to follow her and succeeded in getting the money to
travel with Georgio. Before he did so he wrote a typical angry schoolboy letter to Nora berating her for being "*unjust*" to him, adding "*It is
a monstrous thing to say that you seem to forget me in five days and
to forget the beautiful days of our love*". From Galway Nora wrote
playfully to her '*child*':
"*My darling Jim, Since I left Trieste I am continually thinking about
you how are you getting on without me or do you miss me at all. I am
dreadfully lonely for you. I am quite tired of Ireland already*".

James called on Yeats in London and also on Joseph Hone of the London office of Maunsel & Co. The latter told him that he could do nothing for him about *Dubliners* and to see Roberts in Dublin. He wrote to Stan on 17 July,

> *4 Bowling Green,*
> *Saw Yeats in London. For a wonder he was polite, gave me tea and Georgio fruit*

James arrived in Dublin and had a first meeting with Roberts without any success before he headed to Galway and Nora. There he calmed down and participated in rowing on the river Corrib, cycled through Connemara as far as Clifden, attended the Galway Races at Ballybrit. He and Michael Healy sailed out into Galway Bay landing at Kilronan on the largest of the Aran Islands. Peter Costello writes that Healy showed Joyce the intended site of the transatlantic harbour, adding *"this interested Joyce the nationalist – the tentacles of Ireland reaching round the world, and ironically supplying England in time of war"*[90]. James visited the graveyard at Oughterard and also the site of Michael Bodkin's grave at Rahoon .

He had an article on his trip published in Il Piccolo della Sera on 5 September; *The lazy Dubliner who travels little and knows his own country only by hearsay, believes that the inhabitants of Galway are descendants of Spanish stock and that you can't go four steps without meeting the true Spanish type, with olive complexion and raven hair. The Dubliner is right and wrong .Today in Galway the black eyes are scarce enough, and the raven hair, too, since a titian-red predominates for the most part. The old Spanish houses are falling to ruins, and clumps of weeds grow in the protruding bay windows.*

---

[90] . Costello Peter, *James Joyce- The Years of Growth 1882-1915, a Biography* Kyle Cathie Limited,1992. P. 297.

Outside the city walls grow the suburbs…but you have only to close your eyes to this bothersome city for a moment to see in the twilight of history the 'Spanish City'"[91]

James later wrote on Nora's old boyfriend, the make-believe Michael-Bodkin Furey, who would feature so movingly in *The Dead*, as Nora's tragic boy-friend. He wrote, *"She is Magdalen who weeps remembering the loves she could not return"*. He also began to compos the poem:

She Weeps Over Rahoon"

Rain on Rahoon falls softly, softly falling,
Where my dark lover lies.
Sad is his voice that calls me, sadly calling,
At grey moonrise.

Love, hear thou
How soft, how sad his voice is ever calling
Ever unanswered, and the dark rain falling,
Then as now.

Dark too our hearts, O love, shall lie and cold
As his sad heart has lain
Under the moongrey nettles, the black mould
And muttering rain.

James returned again to Dublin and saw Roberts, accompanied by Padraic Column for support[92]. His earlier letter in *Sinn Fein* had made no difference as Roberts still demanded cuts in the story about King Edward VII. Roberts demanded an indemnity against libel actions of £1,000 which was an impossibility for James, who sought out old friends for support and advice. James sensibly visited his old friend

---

[91] .Ellmann *Critical Writings* p. 229
[92] .Geber Davies Stan, *James Joyce*, Granada 1982 p. 226.

Tom Kettle who had been published by Maunsel. Kettle had also recommended Maunsel as official printer and publisher to University College Dublin. James had attended Kettle's bachelor party after spending hours drinking with Kettle. The Kettles had spent some days visiting the Joyces in Trieste during their honeymoon. But when Kettle read the manuscript he sided entirely with the publisher. He was entirely put off by the two boys meeting with the pederast in '*An Encounter*'[93]. He told James, "*I'll slate that book*". James wrote to Nora in Galway '*of the book I have written which I have carried for years and years in the womb of the imagination as you carried in your womb the children you love, and of how I had fed it day after day out of my brain and my memory*"[94].

Arthur Griffith '*received me very kindly*'

Among those he called on in Dublin was Arthur Griffith. On 26 August he wrote from Dublin to his brother Stanislaus, "*Roberts now wants every proper name changed. I refused to destroy my book… I went then to Griffith who received me very kindly and remembered my letter [17/8/1911 in Sinn Fein]. He says I am not the first person from whom he has heard this story. He says Roberts has been playing that game for years. He says the idea of Maunsel suing me is simple bluff and believes that they will not come into court and that if I get a strong solicitor on my side they will yield. He gave me a note to a first class solicitor in Westmoreland St. He asked me to send him copies of my articles in Il Piccolo della Sera*".

Joyce agreed a price of thirty pounds for the sheets of Dubliners with a view to publishing it himself. But the printer Falconer would not hand them over and despite Joyce's entreaties destroyed them on 11 September. Though the final printed pages were destroyed by

[93] . Lyons JB, the Enigma of Tom kettle Glendale 1983. P. 325n3.
[94] . Maddox Brenda p. 168.

Falconer's, James retained proofs from this printing, and the printing of the first edition of Dubliners in 1914, was based on these. So although the Dublin printing was destroyed, it still played a role in the final publication of the book.

James wrote to Stan on 20 August from Dublin, *Interviewed Roberts today: two hours; result nil.*

He asked Nora to join him in Dublin for Horse Show Week and a visit to the Abbey Theatre. This she did and very soon she was anxious to return to Trieste and escape from James' Aunt Josephine Murray and her daughters.

During that visit James told Griffith that he realised Griffith was seeking to free the Irish people economically and politically and that he Joyce was seeking to liberate them spiritually in his novel. As Richard Ellmann observes, *"Joyce was pleased to be treated as a man having a common cause, though working in a less obviously political medium. For he had remained faithful to his goal of creating new Irishmen and Irishwomen through the honesty and scorching candour of his writing. Ulysses creates new Irishmen to live in Griffith's new State".* Indeed Andras Ungar's book *" Joyce's Ulysses as National Epic: Epic Mimesis and the Political History of the Irish Nation State",* sees *Ulysses* as responding to the Irish Literary Revival's expectation that a native epic would crown Ireland's literary achievements and to the country's imminent independence under Sinn Fein[95]. Ungar argues that Joyce's *Ulysses* is the Irish national epic – a new national epic written at the moment of the new nation, the Irish Free State, was being founded, and one that evades the potential constraints of the epic tradition in order to draw attention instead to what Ungar calls *" the change required in Ireland's too formulaic self-definition".* He writes how Ireland's accession to political

---

[95] . Ungar Andras, *Joyce's Ulysses as National epic* University Press Florida 2002.

sovereignty figures in the compositional design of *Ulysses*. He explores the parallel between the program of Sinn Fein founder Arthur Griffith and the meetings of Stephen Daedalus and Leopold Bloom, with their dreams of self-expression and continuity. Ungar adds a wealth of valuable new detail to the relation of Joyce's Ireland and Leopold's Bloom's Hungary, which is central to his argument, and links Molly Bloom to Stephen Daedalus' focus on the issue of national identity.

James left Dublin for the last time on 11 September 1912 accompanied by Nora and the children. The sheets of Dubliners were destroyed that day by guillotining and pulping by the printer Falconer, according to George Roberts.

As a retort James wrote and circulated '*Gas from a Burner*'.

Ladies and gents, you are here assembled
To hear why earth and heaven trembled
Because of the black and sinister arts
Of an Irish writer in foreign parts.
He sent me a book ten years ago;
I read it a hundred times or so,
Backwards and forwards, down and up,
Through both ends of a telescope,
I printed it all to the very last word
But by the mercy of the Lord
The darkness of my mind was rent
And I saw the writer's foul intent
But I owe a duty to Ireland;
I hold her honour in my hand
This lovely land that always sent
Her writers and artists to banishment

And in a spirit of Irish fun
Betrayed her own leaders, one by one,
'Twas Irish humour, wet and dry,
Flung quicklime into Parnell's eye...
I printed poets, sad silly and solemn...
But I draw the line at that bloody fellow
That was over here dressed in Austrian yellow,
Spouting Italian by the hour
To O'Leary Curtis and John Wyse Power
And writing of Dublin, dirty and drear
, In a manner no blackamoor printer could bear.
Shite and onions! Do you think I'll print
The name of the Wellington Monument
Sydney Parade and Sandymount Tram,
Downes's cake shop and Williams jam?
I'm damned if I do - damned to blazes!
Talk about Irish Names of places!

His father's reaction to it according to Charles Joyce was, *"He's an out and out ruffian without the spark of a gentleman about him"*

Joyce made this comparative moral judgement between himself and those left behind in Dublin, *"What is certain is that I am more virtuous than all that lot - I, who am a real monogamist and have never loved but once in my life"*[96].

James wrote to Yeats on 19 September 1912, *"I suppose you will have heard of the fate of my book Dubliners. Roberts refused to publish it and finally agreed to sell me the first edition for £30 so that I might publish it myself. Then the printer refused to hand over the*

[96]. Ellmann Richard p. 338

1000 copies he had printed either to me or to anyone else andactually broke up the type and burned the whole edition".

 George Roberts was a Protestant Unionist from Belfast and was an actor in the Abbey Theatre and a part of the Irish literary revival. He co-founded Maunsel with Stephen Gwynn and Joseph Maunsel Hone. He published Yeats, Synge, Lady Gregory AE Russell, James Stephens and Douglas Hyde. He had good reason to reject *Dubliners* as it could have led to cases of libel against the Company. He was one of the very many people who had loaned money to Joyce which was never repaid. He was also one of the men who had thrown the drunken Joyce out of the entry to the Camden Theatre as written about in *Ulysses*. Many of the characters in the stories were readily identifiable in a small city like Dublin. Vigilance Committee were not unheard of either. The printer Falconer was a State employee and did a lot of printing for Catholic Societies[97].

---

[97] . McCourt p. 273. Stanislaus Joyce to Constantine Curran 2 march 1955.

Chapter 8.

THE WONDER WORKER EZRA POUND

TRIESTE 1912

Fortune favoured Joyce back in Trieste and his income became more steady. He got a morning job at the Scuola Superiore di Commercio Revoltella and taught his private pupils in the afternoons. These enjoyed his informal ways and conversational approach to teaching English. Romantic thoughts between teacher and pupils led to many new poems between 1912-1916, especially *'his real or concocted relationship with one Signorina Popper*[98].

James also was invited to give a series of lectures to the most prestigious cultural association in Trieste, the Societa di Minerva. James wished to Hibernicise Europe and Europeanise Ireland. *Il Piccolo* reported after his first lecture, *'Prof. James Joyce, whom our intellectual world knows and admires as a thinker, a writer, and a journalist, began his cycle of 10 lectures on Shakespeare's Hamlet in the completely packed Minerva Hall'*. After his final lecture the same paper wrote, ' *Yesterday evening Dr. James Joyce concluded his*

---

[98] . Donoghue Denis, *Essays on Irish literature* 1988. P. 115.

series of lectures in English on Hamlet…Joyce was thanked by his audience who gave him a warm and prolonged round of applause"[99].

An unexpected letter from publishers Grant Richards arrived in late 1913, asking to see *Dubliners* again. James wrote Grant Richards on 22 November 1913, Dubliners *printed completely and entire edition of one thousand copies burned by publisher. A complete set of proofs is in my possession. I am prepared to contribute towards the expenses of publication.*

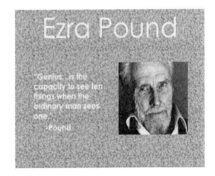

---

[99] . McCourt p. 192.

IMPORTANT LETTER FROM 'WONDERWORKER'

DUBLINERS FINALLY PUBLISHED

Another unexpected letter from a friend of WB Yeats, Ezra Pound, offered to act as an unpaid go-between for James to get material, especially poetry, published in various journals and magazines. The letter said,

15 December 1913

Dear Sir,

Mr. Yeats has been speaking to me of your writing. I am informally connected with a couple of new and impecunious paper. I am bonae voluntatis,---don't in the least know that I can be of any use to you...[100].

Pound was an American recently arrived in England and a fan of WB Yeats. He had become literary editor of the *Egoist* under the editorship of Harriet Weaver. An agreement that Joyce's *Portrait of the Artist as a Young Man* was to be serialised from 2 February followed and he had to work zealously to finish each chapter as required. His sudden change of fortune and resulting publicity saw him demand an immediate decision from Grant Richards on *Dubliners*. The subsequent positive response from Grant Richards was modified by a contract offering no royalties on the first 500 copies with Joyce himself having to take 120 copies. The book of 1250 copies, was published on 15 June 1914. It was well reviewed in the *Egoist* and *New Statesman*, though described as '*cynical*'

---

[100] *.Letters of Ezra Pound to James Joyce* Forrest Read ed. 1967 pp17-18

'pointless' 'sterile'. James presented a few copies to friends *"but for the most part he made people pay for it"[101]*. The outbreak of war caused postal problems for a time but Joyce was at last on a successful writing wave as he completed *Exiles* and began *Ulysses*. He relished the attention that he was getting in promotional terms by Pound and Weaver's efforts in London.

Declan Kiberd wrote of *Dubliners*: *each of the stories in Dubliners chronicles an abortive attempt at freedom, an attempt which is doomed precisely because it couches itself in the forms and languages of the enemy, and this becomes a prophecy of the failure of a nationalism which would insist on confining its definitions to the categories designed by the coloniser[102]*.

WORLD WAR ONE

On 17 September 1914 James was suspended without pay from his School. He appealed this and on 8 January 1915 the Inspector wrote, " *I believe that the renewal of Joyce's contract would be a very good thing, that he is a quiet individual who worries, above all, about making a living"*. This was communicated to James on 13 March. Though this episode caused James great financial distress his brother fared much worse. Stanislaus Joyce had become publicly involved in political affairs and was well known to the authorities. When war broke out he did not remain quiet but continued to act publicly. He

---

[101]. McCourt p. 216.
[102]. Kiberd, *Inventing Ireland* p. 330

was arrested on 9 January 1915 and interned in an Austrian camp for the duration of the war. James continued to teach. He confided to a friend, "*My political faith can be expressed in a word: Monarchies, constitutional or unconstitutional, disgust me. Kings are mountebanks. Republics are slippers for everyone's feet. Temporal power is gone and good riddance. What else is left? Can we hope for monarchy by divine right? Do you believe in the Sun of the Future?* James feared violence as air raids and canon fire forced him to consider escape. His school closed and his private pupils gradually disappeared. His sister Eileen married a Czech bank cashier in Trieste in April 1915, with James acting as best man in an oversized borrowed dress suit. His father wrote to him expressing satisfaction that "*both you and your brother will look to her future and see that she does not take any step that may mar her future*".

Italy entered the war in May 1915 and as the large Italian population in Trieste became a potential trouble spot, the authorities partially evacuated the city turning it into an armed camp. James had to leave but where to? He succeeded in getting a visa and used his pupil contacts to be allowed by the Austrians to leave for neutral Switzerland, on condition that he would not engage in any activity against the Emperor. He travelled on 27 June 1915, leaving his furniture and books in his flat as the family decided to leave as quickly as possible lest circumstances worsen. James paid little income tax in Trieste as the tax collector was an admirer of his. When a new tax collector demanded he pay James stopped smoking until he had deprived the government of an equal amount of money in tobacco tax[103].

---

[103] . Ellmann Richard *James Joyce* p. 386

In Zurich as usual Joyce had no money, but his network of friends and relations continued to support him. Michael Healy, Nora's Uncle and an admirer of James' writings, sent them £9 from Galway after James wrote seeking help, to tide them over initially. Zurich was in great contrast to Trieste. It was clean, orderly, and secure. In London WB Yeats approached Edmund Gosse for assistance for Joyce. He wrote, *"I have just heard that James Joyce, an Irish poet and novelist of whose fine talent I can easily satisfy you, is in probably great penury through the war. He was in Trieste teaching English and has now arrived at Zurich. He has children and a wife. If things are as I believe, would it be possible for him to be given a grant from the Royal Literary Fund?"* Gosse wrote on Joyce's behalf but carped to Yeats that neither Yeats nor Joyce had offered any loyalty to the Allies in the war. Yeats replied, wishing the Allies victory saying *"I thank you very much for what you have done; but it never occurred to me that it was necessary to express sympathy 'Frank 'or otherwise with the cause of the Allies. I certainly wish them victory and as I have never known Joyce to agree with his neighbours in Austria, has probably made his sympathy as frank as you could wish. I never asked my friend about it in any of the few notes I have sent him. He has never had anything to do with Irish politics, extreme or otherwise, and I think he dislikes politics. He always seemed to me to have only literary and philosophic sympathies. To such men the Irish atmosphere brings isolation, not anti-English feeling. I again thank you for what you have done for this man of genius"*.

Yeats then wrote himself to the Fund praising Joyce's *"beautiful gift"* in *Chamber Music* and *Dubliners. I have read in the Egoist certain chapters of a new novel, a disguised autobiography, which increased my conviction that he is the most remarkable new talent in Ireland today*"[104]. Joyce himself then had to write in July stating his financial position. He said he received no income from his writings, yet incurred great expenses. He stated his debts as circa 600 Austrian Crowns. Ezra Pound also wrote on his behalf to the Fund. Joyce was awarded £75 over nine months. He had entered the promising world of patronage.

In September 1916 James wrote to Yeats,

"Dear Yeats,
Ezra Pound wrote to me telling me of your kindness in writing a letter of recommendation on my behalf as a result of which a royal bounty has been granted to me (£100)...I can never thank you enough for having brought me into relations with your friend Ezra Pound who is indeed a wonder worker"

John Quinn.

Zurich had an inhospitable climate compared to Trieste which caused James and Nora many health problems, especially ongoing eye problems for him, as he worked at home almost entirely. Michael Healy advised James to carry a potato in his pocket to ward

---

[104] . *Letters of WB Yeats* p 596-600

off his rheumatism. Joyce did so and had Leopold Bloom do likewise[105]. James received £50 from Harriet Weaver in 1915, ostensibly as royalties as he told her "*I am writing a book, Ulysses*". In 1916 John Quinn the Irish-American lawyer became a patron.

Ezra Pound had again pursued arrangements for another award for Joyce through a Civil list grant. This came to £100 from the British Civil List, as referred to in above letter, courtesy of Edward Marsh private secretary of Prime Minister Asquith. George Moore was one of the people contacted for a reference for Joyce. He admired in particular '***The Dead***', "*which seemed to me perfection. I regretted that I was not the author*". Moore added that "*Joyce left a disagreeable reputation behind him in Dublin, but he came back after some years a different man and everything I heard of him is to his credit. Of his political views I know nothing. He was not in Ireland during the sowing of the Sinn Fein seed and I hope that he is not even a home ruler. Democratic principles are unsuited to Ireland...The Irish like priests and believe in the power of the priests to forgive them their sins and to change God into a biscuit. ..P.S. I am sure from a literary point of view Joyce is deserving of help*[106]. James had become a famous writer and so recognised by the English establishment.

The first English publication of *Portrait of the Artist as a Young Man* took place ostensibly on 29 December 1916 by BW Huebsch in New York. Joyce wanted it published in 1916 to allow *Exiles* to be

---

[105] . Maddox Brenda p. 198. This mention of a potato has provided a field day for writers seeking to interpret Joyce in all his works and pomps, particularly the significance of it referring obliquely to the Famine in Ireland which was only one generation away from Joyce. It brings to mind Joyce's statement that he had put in so many enigmas and puzzles that it will keep the professors busy for centuries arguing over what he meant, and that's the only way of insuring one's immortality.

[106] . Ellmann p. 406.

published in 1917. Huebsch wrote to Harriet Weaver, *"I got just enough copies from the bindery to make it possible for me truthfully to say that the book was published. The distribution to the bookshops and reviewers will be made this month of January"*. The Egoist Press published it on 12 February, after buying 1,768 sheets from Ben Huebsch, receiving them on 22 January[107].

Portrait saw Joyce recognised as a writer of important literature, with a laudatory review from the famous HG Wells saying *"is as good as the last book of Gulliver's Travels. One conversation in the book is a superb success, the one in which Mr Dedalus carves the Christmas turkey; I write with all due deliberation that Sterne himself could not have done it better"*. Edward Garnett, a reader for Duckworth Publications, was critical, writing James Joyce's *'Portrait of the Artist as a Young Man' wants going through carefully from start to finish. There are many 'longueurs [boring passages]. Passages which, though the publisher's reader may find them entertaining, will be tedious to the ordinary man among the reading public. Though ably written it is too discursive, formless, unstrained and ugly things, ugly words are too prominent; shoved in ones face, on purpose, unnecessarily. The point of view will be voted 'a little sordid', and at the end the book there is a complete falling to bits. The author shows he has art, strength and originality but this manuscript wants time and trouble spent on it"*. This critique drew a furious response from Ezra Pound to JB Pinker, HG Well's agent[108].

It was April before there was a notable review in one of the Irish newspapers, the *Freeman's Journal*. It was headed, *'A Dyspeptic Portrait'* and read, "Mr. Joyce's prose is masterly in its terseness and force, even his most *casual descriptions haunt the mind by their*

[107] . Geber Stan James Joyce Granada.p. 248.
[108] . ibid p. 241.

vividness and wonderful economy of line. What he sees he can reproduce in words with a precision as rare as it is subtle; the pity is that, in one of his own phrases, the memory of these things has too often 'coated his palate with the scum of disgust'. Yeats sent Maud Gonne a copy of *Portrait.* She responded on 16 March 1916, "*I have read Joyce's book. – I read it with weariness & difficulty, it seemed to me so deadly dull- It sent me to sleep several evenings. I struggled on with it because of what you said and generally, even when I may not like I admire what you recommend. The childhood part was the best. One can understand a child being articulate & searchingly hesitant – it may develop something interesting , but when that goes on indefinitely into manhood, one wonders why it was worth anyone's while writing dreary chapters about him, or worthwhile reading them. There is no character vividly drawn except the careless and self-satisfied drunken father. I think Willie that you have not read the book. There are little bits of coarseness dragged in unnecessarily, because so called realist writers who seem to me to miss the real essence of life, think they may get an effect by shocking their readers which will make them forget the monotonous dullness of the pages. To have lived in Dublin and seen but its ugliness & squalor, to have associated with those eagerly intense living people & to have been able to describe nothing but dull futility & boredom seems to denote a nature to whom the stars would look like bits of tinsel paper. Tell me the truth – confess- you have not read the book yourself. Pound perhaps has read you extracts – isn't that so?[109]*

Due to ongoing health problems the Joyce family moved to the milder climate of Locarno for the winter of 1917, where James became

---

[109] . MacBride White Anna & Norman Jeffares, *The Gonne-Yeats Letters*, Pimlico. 1993. p. 368

infatuated with a tall 26 year old German woman Dr. Gertrude Kaempffer, who did not respond to his overtures[110]. Nora wrote to him in August about Locarno, "*It was quite lovely to hear the men calling out the prices and making as much noise as they could just like in Trieste; they are just like Italians lively and dirty and disorderly; it is quite different from Zurich*".

Stanislaus wrote in some desperation about their accommodation in Trieste, "*Your quarter has been kept for you for six months in spite of shortage of flats in Trieste. I have paid the rent. Some eight years agoI took the quarter for you, moved in and paid the first rent. Now I have paid the last rent for you and moved out. It has cost me dearly 300 lire. I have just emerged from four years of hunger and am in squalor,trying to get on my feet again. Do you think you can give me a rest?*" In September James accommodation needs in Trieste were identified as "*a flat of six rooms with bath and electric light*".

---

[110] . Maddox Brenda p. 205.

CHAPTER 9.

PATRONAGE PAYS

Back in Zurich James discovered on 27 February 1918 that a female admirer, who believed him to be a literary genius, had deposited 12,000 Swiss Francs in an account to be paid out to him in monthly instalments of 1,000 francs[111]. She was Mrs Edith Rockefeller McCormack a philanthropist daughter of John D. Rockefeller who had been living in Zurich since 1913. He visited her to thank her for her benefaction. She replied, *"I know you are a great artist"*. Joyce was persuaded to invest some of the money in a theatrical group he and Claud Sykes had founded in Zurich named *The English Players*. Joyce was keen to have his play *Exiles* performed.

---

[111] .Maddox Brenda p. 207.

FRANK BUDGEN

The best friend that Joyce made on the continent was Frank Budgen. He was a self-educated Englishman who worked at the Ministry of Information in Zurich. He was a painter, a model for the sculptor August Suter, and open to Joyce's innovative work. They first met at a dinner party in Zurich. Joyce soon began to recover his old companionableness. As James became close friends with Budgen and August Suter and his wife, Nora, though at first disapproving, later began to join their socialising. She began to realise that, despite her earlier lack of interest, her husband must be involved in a worthwhile enterprise. She had grown immune to listening to her husband going on about his writing, and was supremely indifferent to it. But she observed that these others never appeared to get bored listening to James. In a way this may have been positive for their relationship as she coped with his many frailties of character. James realised this only too well and told Budgen "*My wife's personality is absolute proof against any influence of mine*" though confessing that he loved her dearly. Once when James asked Budgen to nominate one "*complete all-round character presented by any writer*", Budgen nominated Jesus. James responded, "*He was a bachelor, and never lived with a woman. Surely living with a woman is one of the most difficult things a man has to do, and he never did it*"[112]. Joyce of course nominated Ulysses/Leopold Bloom.

---

[112] . Budgen Frank, *James Joyce and the Making of Ulysses* p. 17-19

DUBLIN AND EAST TOURISM

HERE, IN JOYCE'S IMAGINATION
WAS BORN IN MAY 1866
LEOPOLD BLOOM
CITIZEN, HUSBAND, FATHER, WANDERER
REINCARNATION OF ULYSSES

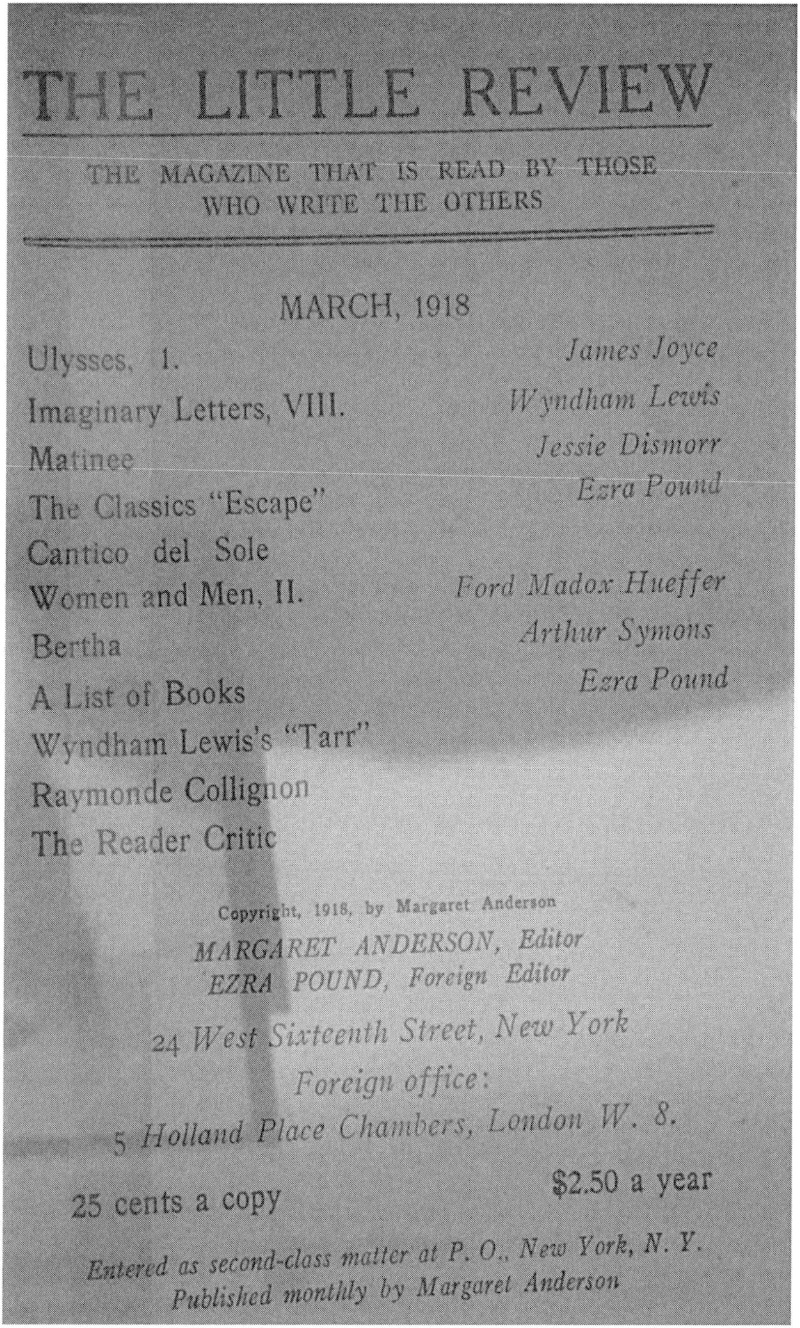

THE LITTLE REVIEW

THE MAGAZINE THAT IS READ BY THOSE
WHO WRITE THE OTHERS

MARCH, 1918

MARGARET ANDERSON, *Editor*

EZRA POUND, *Foreign Editor*

24 *West Sixteenth Street, New York*

Foreign office:

5 *Holland Place Chambers, London W. 8.*

25 cents a copy $2.50 a year

Entered as second-class matter at P. O., New York, N. Y.
Published monthly by Margaret Anderson

James' novel *Ulysses* was then being serialised in *The Little Review* and gaining attention. His mentor Ezra Pound foresaw difficulties with its crudity and tried unsuccessfully to have James change such features in the book, but he warmed to the character of Leopold Bloom. He wrote to Joyce, *"Bloom is a great man, and you have almightily answered the critics who asked me whether having made Stephen, more or less autobiography, you could ever go on and create a second character…"*. Harriet Weaver then began to serialise it in The *Egoist* and soundings about publishing the entire book were taken.

MARTHE FLEISCHMANN

In late 1918 James again became infatuated with another attractive lady who had a limp and lived nearby. She reminded him of that female figure walking into the sea at Dollymount sixteen years earlier, with her skirts up around her waist, which had infiltrated his mind forever more. He wrote in Scene Four of *Exiles* "Is *she the same girl I saw on the beach in Ireland in 1898? Her skirts stuck up her bloomers as she waded in the Irish Sea. Beckoning me. Beckoning me to a life that has no separation from body or soul*". Yeats rejected this play writing to Joyce, *"I did not recommend your play to the Irish Theatre because it is a type of work we have never played well. It is too far from the folk drama*". James began to stalk Marthe furtively, as he thought in a voyeuristic fashion, but she knew what was afoot and enjoyed the attention. Her name was Marthe Fleischmann and she was Swiss. Eventually James wrote to her telling her how she resembled his image from Dollymount. When she later discovered that he was a famous writer she replied, and a perverted surreptitious correspondence ensued. She was a kept mistress and James didn't tell his wife. He could spy on Marthe from his flat and she enjoyed his attention. He involved a doubting Frank Budgen in the escapades as he procured an erotic present for Marthe to view. Whether any physical sexual contact occurred between them is unknown. James told Budgen "*I have explored the coldest and hottest parts of a woman's body*". Budgen 's view was that Marthe may have been fingered at most by James[113]. Peter Costello writes that of it as "*an affair that was consummated*"[114] Matters reached an unexpected state when Marthe's lover wrote to Joyce telling him that Marthe was hospitalised with a manic attack. She had confessed her liaison with Joyce and blamed him for her state of mind. James had to meet the lover and was able to reassure him convincingly *a la Bloom* that nothing had happened between them. As always, James made full use out of this bizarre experience in *Ulysses* in the Circe and Nausicaä episodes, as he had Leopold Bloom write secretly to Martha Clifford. This episode became public only when Marthe sold her letters after Joyce's death[115].

A German banker and Jewish friend of James' named Ottocaro Weiss became very close to Nora, who was a very attractive woman, and may have had an affair with Weiss at this time. James refused to accept any explanation from Weiss whom he saw as just another who betrayed his trust.

Brenda Maddox surmises that Joyce may have become impotent and as a result "*the only climax in Ulysses comes from an act of masturbation*" by Bloom as he spies Gerty McDowell revealing her knickers on Sandymount Strand amid the long scatological scene, as all the time *through the open window of the church the fragrant incense was wafted and with it the fragrant names of her who was*

[113] .*Times Literary Supplement* 12/12/1975 'facts, fictions and fadographs' Budgen to JS Atherton.
[114] . Costello p. 9.
[115] . Maddox Brenda p. 219.

conceived without stain of original sin…Gerty could picture the wholescene in the church as, the stained glass windows lighted up, the candles , the flowers and the blue banners of the blessed Virgin's sodality and Father Conroy was helping Canon O'Hanlon at the altar, carrying things in and out with his eyes cast down, as Canon O'Hanlon conducts Benediction in Star of the Sea Church[116]. As Gerty eventually moves along the strand, *it was darker now and there were stones and bits of wood on the strand and slippy seaweed. She walked with a certain quiet dignity characteristic of her but with care and very slowly because Gerty was…Tight boots? No. she's lame O! Mr. Bloom watched her as she limped away. Poor girl! That's why she's left on the shelf and the others did a sprint. Thought something was wrong by the cut of her jib. Jilted beauty. A defect is ten times worse in a woman. But makes them polite glad I didn't know when she was on show. Hot little devil all the same. Wouldn't mind.*

Stanley Price comments, "*Joyce had stored away Marthe Fleischmann's handicap in Zurich for Gerty McDowell's exit at Sandymount Strand*"[117].Edna O'Brien writes, "*Gerty MacDowell on Sandymount Strand, her yellow flower punishing Leopold Bloom's man flower was a mere prologue to the appetites of Molly Bloom, a woman exceeding all habits and hunger*"[118].

---

[116] . ibid p. 221. Canon O'Hanlon, 1821-1905, was Parish Priest in Sandymount from 1880-1905. He was a native of Stradbally Co.Laois and the author of a two volume History of Queens County. He is remembered in Sandymount today by the Canon O'Hanlon Memorial Boys National l School. The beach is no longer directly behind the Church as a large infill has created a public park on that location. On his last visits to Ireland Joyce was offered the post of 'Cantor' at Star of the Sea Church.

[117] . Price Stanley, p. 150.

[118] . O'Brien Edna, *James Joyce*, Weidenfeld & Nicholson 1999. p. 91.

The author stands, where James Joyce stood Leopold Bloom, facing onto Sandymount Strand opposite Leahy's Terrace, with Star of the Sea Church in the background. Joyce had been offered the post of cantor in the Church in 1912.

 Canon O'Hanlon P.P.

Canon O'Hanlon Memorial Hall, Star of Sea School, Sandymount

Chapter 10.

HOME RULE AND EASTER RISING

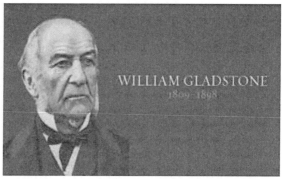

James Joyce had written in 1907 that William Gladstone was a hypocrite who pretended an interest in Home Rule because he knew that the House of Lords would veto the Bill in the Commons. Joyce held that the Liberals and Tory Catholics were as unreliable as the Irish Parliamentary Party [IPP]. He wrote, *"The Irish Parliamentary Party has gone broke. For twenty-seven years it has talked and agitated politically. In that time it has collected 35 million Francs from its followers, and the fruit of its agitation is that Irish taxes have gone up 88 million francs and the Irish population has lessened a million. The representatives have enlarged their own lot, aside from small worries like a few months in prison and some lengthy sessions. From the sons of average citizens, traders, and legal representative without clients they have become well-paid syndics, managers of factories and commercial houses, newspapers owners. They have*

given proof of their compassion only in 1891 when they sold their leader, Parnell, to the pharisiacal conscience of the English Dissenters without extracting the thirty pieces of silver" He averred that the only hope for Ireland lay with Arthur Griffith's Sinn Fein and passive and economic resistance. Joyce thought highly of the weapon of the 'boycott'.

Joyce had also cast his cynical eye on political developments after the General Election of December 1910 and was not impressed. He saw Asquith, Balfour and Redmond as *'foolish leaders'*. Lloyd George was *'warlike'*. He found the Radicals conservative and the Conservatives radical, wishing to transfer power from Parliament to the people in plebiscites. The clerical Irish Party became part of the anti-clerical and illiberal government. Chamberlain Gladstonian Liberalism went to Imperialism while Churchill went in the opposite direction. He was cynical about the Parliament Law making such an immediate ground breaking difference to Ireland, so diverse was the Government. The Election of 1910 resulted in the Liberals and Unionists tying with 272 seats each, with the Labour Party having 47 seats and the IPP 84 seats. Joyce was sceptical enough to foresee Parliament reduce Irish representation by half to avoid granting Home Rule. He said that despite Ireland becoming part of British democratic life she has never been faithful to England nor to herself, as she discarded her own language for English, betrayed her stars and served only the Catholic Church[119]. For Joyce, his loyalty to James Stephens, and his obsessive neurosis with the betrayal of Parnell by the Irish Parliamentary Party, sent him *"in to unreason"* as he compared John Dillon to Lord Castlereagh, who was the architect of the Act of Union in 1801. He used the Parnell myth to protect his own artistic role in Irish life. In *Portrait of an Artist* Joyce has Stephen Dedalus say to the

---

[119] . *Critical Writings*, Mason & Ellmann p. 196, 209-213; Barry Kevin pp. 142-144, 155-158.

nationalist Davin, *"No honourable and sincere man has given up to you his life and his youth and his affection from the days of Tone to those of Parnell but you sold him to the enemy or failed him in need or reviled him and left him for another. And you invite me to be one of you. I'll see you damned first".*

What was sought for Ireland under Home Rule was a repetition of what Sinn Fein had stood for from its beginning, as had been sought by James Joyce in 1907, when he demanded that the power over legislation, taxes, the police, the Supreme Court, and the Agrarian Commission were fundamental

Joyce was as usual sceptical in 1912 when the Home Rule Bill was passed. He looked at it from the viewpoint of the bourgeois that he was, noting that despite Irish nationalist effusion; Britain would as usual control taxes. In two years the old Irish Parliament would reopen, with the ghost of Parnell looking on. While elaborating on apparent deficiencies in Parnell's profile and listing examples of his disdain for public acclaim, Joyce places him far above Disraeli and Gladstone's Liberal elasticity. He recalled once again that when Parnell refused to resign at Gladstone's insistence, only 8 of his 83 colleagues supported him, as the Irish press and clergy destroyed their *'uncrowned King'*, aged forty five.

JOYCE THE REPUBLICAN, DEMANDS A REVOLUTION

James Joyce had long supported Arthur Griffith's Sinn Fein and even developed a republican stance. Declan Kiberd said that *"Joyce wrote from the viewpoint of a staunch republican"*[120]. Herbert Gorman

---

[120] . Kiberd Declan, Irish Times Supplement on Home Rule 25/4/12012.

wrote, *"Joyce, if anything, was an Irish nationalist at heart"[121]*, Joyce called for a revolution, fed up with all the failures of the fights for freedom. In a lecture in Trieste in 1907 he demanded a successful insurrection though never believing that it would come in his lifetime. He said:

"One thing alone seems obvious to me. It is way past time for Ireland to have done once and for all with failure. If she is truly capable of revitalizing, let her rouse, or let her cover her head and lie down graciously in her grave forever. - - But though the Irish are articulate, an insurrection is not made of human breath and negotiations... If she wants to put on the show for which we have delayed so long, this time, let it be comprehensive, and conclusive. But telling these Irish actors to hurry up, as our forefathers before us told them not so long ago, is hopeless. I, for one, am certain not to see that curtain rise as I shall have already taken the last tram home"

Tom Kettle   *Francis Sheehy Skeffington*

But when the performance of the Rising did unexpectedly occur in Dublin at Easter 1916, Joyce had recently become compromised by *'taking the King's shilling'*, remained quiet. Of course the tragic death of his old friend Sheehy-Skeffington and the partial destruction of

---

[121] . Gorman. p. 186.

Dublin did affect him. The Sheehy family suffered another tragedy when Thomas Kettle was killed fighting in France in September 1916. He wrote a letter of sympathy to the two widowed Sheehy sisters he had known so well, saying *"I am grieved to learn that so many misfortunes have fallen on your family in these evil days"*. As Richard Ellmann writes, *"Joyce followed the events with pity; although he evaluated the Rising as useless, he felt also out of things"*[122]. Later in 1918 he was glad when the British had to abandon their plan to introduce conscription to Ireland, remarking *'Erin go bragh'*. At that stage he looked forward to the time when he would revisit an independent Ireland. When Kathleen Cruise O'Brien's husband died suddenly a fund was raised in 1928 to pay the fees of their son, Conor, to remain at Sandford Park School. Among the contributors was James Joyce[123].

Joyce in Dublin.   O'Connell St Dublin.

Joyce got heavily involved in staging a successful performance of Oscar Wilde's *The Importance of Being Earnest* in Zurich in 1918. In the excitement of being congratulated he shouted out, *"Hurrah for Ireland. Poor Wilde was Irish and so am I"*[124]. As often happened with James, financial and libel disagreements with the leading actor, Henry Carr, meant the episode ended in legal proceedings with him

[122] . Ellmann p. 399.
[123] . Akenson. P. 77.
[124] . ibid p. 426.

taking two actions to the courts in late 1918. The English Consul became an enemy of Joyce and the players group, as James became pro-German. The actors group, *the English Players* which had been founded by Joyce and Claud Sykes continued to produce plays and Nora played a starring role in one of their production. James, as usual for him, wrote unsuccessfully to Prime Minister Lloyd George and the British Minister in Berne about the dispute. He became embroiled in a legal case which caused him agitation and fifty francs for settlement. A friend who heard of this fine sent him $700.

His financial worries eased in 1919 when a letter from Nora told him that a donor was about to invest a large sum of money for his direct benefit. Having wealthy benefactors made life easier for James and his family. When Miss Weaver and Ezra Pound sought to interfere in his continuing writing and publishing of the instalments of *Ulysses*, he resisted them, writing to Weaver, *"During the last two years when I have received your gifts I have always had the foreboding (now proved false) that each episode of the book as it advanced would alienate gradually the sympathy of the person who was helping me"*.

When Mrs McCormack wanted him to submit to analysis by Jung, he told a friend, *"it was unthinkable"*. This led to Mrs McCormick ending her subsidy to him. He asked to meet her but she resisted, writing, *"As the bank told you, I am not able to help you any longer financially, but now that the difficult years of the war are past, you will find publishers and will come forward yourself, I know"*. As usual James believed that some one of his friends had betrayed him. Since Weiss was a friend of Jung and without any evidence and despite his earnest denials, he blamed Otto Weiss for influencing his Patron over his repeated refusals to deal with Jung. James was then preparing to leave Zurich and returning to live in Trieste. They arrived there in October 1919 at which time Trieste had become part of Italy. The city was battle-scared as the old charm and sophistication of the old Austro-Hungarian Empire passed away[125]. James soon realised that the "rich and varied elements which had provided him with an invaluable workshop for his writing no longer existed"[126]

 Meanwhile John Quinn the American lawyer and Patron offered $1,000 as a first instalment on the manuscript of *Ulysses*. Stanislaus was freed from internment and returned to Trieste full of bitterness towards James with whom he had little contact during the war years. Eileen Joyce and her husband also returned to Trieste and all lived uncomfortably in a large flat. James consented to teach for one hour a week. He soon began working on *Ulysses* again as he wrote to Aunt Josephine Murray to check an important detail about Gerty McDowell. He asked, *"whether there are trees (and of what kind) behind the Star of the Sea church in Sandymount visible from the shore and also whether there are steps leading down at the side from Leahy's terrace".*

Feeling very much alone with *Ulysses* James wrote to Frank Budgen in Zurich seeking to entice him to visit Trieste. As he finished sections of the novel he sent them to Ezra Pound who sent them to Miss Weaver who was very pleased with the results.

Pound had been eager to meet Joyce and after some difficulties they arranged to meet in Sermione. Joyce wrote to Pound *"it is my intention to travel over that line en route for England and Ireland as soon as possible…My only reason for accepting your invitation to Sermione was to meet you…So I propose to spend three months in Ireland in order to write Circe and the close of the book…My wife and children would stay in Galway. I too there or in Dublin. The disturbed state of Ireland is of course a reason for not going. There*

---

[125] . Price Stanley. P. 147.

[126] . McCourt p. 248.

may be other reasons…I must finish my book in quiet even if I sell off the furniture here". They met in Sermione on 8 June. Joyce was accompanied by Giorgio. Pound wrote to John Quinn, " *Joyce— pleasing; after the first shell of cantankerous Irishman, I got the impression that the real man is the author of Chamber Music, the sensitive. The rest is the genius…A concentration and absorption passing Yeats'- Yeats has never taken on anything requiring the condensation of Ulysses…He is, of course, as stubborn as a mule or an Irishman, but I failed to find him at all unreasonable, Thank god, he has been stubborn enough to know his job and stick to it".*

Generous but anonymous gifts began to come James' way through a firm of solicitors. The initial sum was for £1,500 followed by £2,000, £500 making it all up to £8,500 by early 1921. Discussing who it was with Pound they decided it was a lady. It turned out to be Harriet Weaver and she would continue to support him to the end without making any demands.

Sylvia Beach and Adrienne Monnier

James Joyce & Clovis Monnier

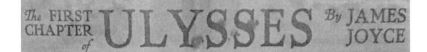

The FIRST CHAPTER of **ULYSSES** By JAMES JOYCE

TWO WORLDS
MONTHLY

*Devoted to the Increase
of the Gaiety of Nations*

Partial Contents of
VOLUME ONE   NUMBER ONE

TWO WORLDS PUBLISHING COMPANY
500 FIFTH AVE., Suite 405-8, NEW YORK

Edited by
Samuel Roth

PRICE FIFTY CENTS

Chapter 11.

ULYSSES PUBLISHED

James now decided to accept Pound's advice that he visit Paris. He
had retrieved the manuscript of *Ulysses* from Mrs MacCormack and
agreed a price with John Quinn. Stanislaus refused to see the Joyces
off from Trieste and the relationship between the brothers never
recovered its closeness. James and family arrived in Paris on 8 July
1920 with stops at Milan and Venice. They supposedly were in Paris
for a short visit before going on to London. Ezra Pound organised
that they were introduced to many admiring parties there and enjoyed
a busy social life. As Paris became a centre of culture again it
attracted many visiting artists, many of whom had to pay social calls
to James. They saw Nora as rather an embarrassment not realising the
essential roles she played for James and their children. Arthur Power
realised that James and Nora understood each other's roles perfectly
as did other Irish visitors[127]. When James met Sylvia Beach at a
social gathering, she asked, *"Is this the great James Joyce?"* He
visited her shop next day, *Shakespeare & Company*. She and her
friend, another bookshop proprietor, Adrienne Monnier christened
him '*Melancholy Jesus & Crooked Jesus*'. He soon became a
celebrity in Paris. He was close to finishing the last episodes of
Ulysses and who was going to publish it became an issue. Printers in
England refused to touch it. BW Huebsch had published several of

---

[127]. Maddox Brenda p. 245.

James' books in America and as interested in publishing the novel. But the American Post Office had destroyed four issues of the *Little Review* because the scene where Bloom masturbates while watching Gerty McDowell on Sandymount strand was deemed obscene. The *Little Review* was prosecuted in America in 1920 where John Quinn, the Irish-American literary patron, defended it. The passage in question was read by the Court in Greenwich Village and Quinn contended that Gerty's exhibition of her drawers were not nearly so flagrant as the skimpy attire of the mannequins in Fifth Avenue. The female editors were fined $50 each for publishing obscenity and forbidden to publish any more instalments of *Ulysses*. Edna O'Brien writes '*How near or how far Bloom and Gerty are from each other, we will never know. It is all in the mind and in the words*'[128].

 Ben Huebsch decided on 5 April 1921 that he could not risk publishing the book, writing to Quinn:

31 Nassau Street, New York City

I send you this note to confirm my attitude towards Joyce's Ulysses. A New York court having held that the publication of a part of this in The Little Review was a violation of the law, I am unwilling to publish the book unless some changes are made in the manuscript as submitted to me by Miss HC Weaver, who represents Joyce in London. In view of your statement that Joyce declines absolutely to make any alterations, I must decline to publish it. I repeat however, that if you or Joyce, or both, conclude that a change of some kind in the manuscript is desirable, I feel that I am entitled to be the first offer of the American rights under those circumstances[129].

John Quinn proposed a private edition of 1,500 copies. Joyce

---

[128] . O'Brien Edna, *James Joyce*, Weidenfeld & Nicholson 1999, p. 116.
[129] .Gorman. p. 277.

informed Miss Beach in Paris saying *"My book will never come out now"*. She replied, *"Would you let Shakespeare & Company have the honour of bringing out your Ulysses?"* James accepted her offer immediately.

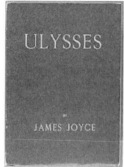 

Joyce with Sylvia Beach at Shakespeare & Co. Paris.

Arthur Power, the young Irishman who wanted to write in a French mode, had met Joyce in Paris. James retorted, *"You are an Irishman and you must write in your own tradition. Borrowed styles are no good. You must write what is in your blood and not what is in your brain"*. When Power said he wanted to be an international writer, Joyce added, *"They were national first and it was the intensity of their own nationalism which made them international in the end...for myself I always write about Dublin, because if I can get to the heart of Dublin I can get to the heart of all the cities of the world"*[130]. James had earlier written in Act Two of *Exiles*;

Joyce ; *There are two ways of thinking , Ottocaro Weiss, the Greek Way and the Jewish way.*

Weiss; And what is the Irish way Mr. Joyce?

Joyce The Irish Way? Jewish of course.

---

[130] . Power Arthur, *An Old Waterford House* p.63-4. + Irish Times, *James Joyce The Man* 30/12/1944.

Schwarz; And why is that? Why is it Jewish Mr. Joyce

Joyce: Because my Dear Schwarz, the Irish like the Jews are impulsive they are given to fantasy. They are associate thinkers ...when they bother to think at all that is ...and they have been found wanting in rational discipline.

Schwarz; Perhaps that is why so far their destinies have been similar as you have been saying Mr. Joyce .

While James was working assiduously on completing *Ulysses* he also continued his drunken ways to the continuing horror of Nora. She tried to tell his companions of the damage being done. James' regular patron, whom he continued to ask for top ups, Harriet Weaver, was horrified when she discovered his regular drunkenness. She wrote to him on the evils of drink. He had been warned himself that his ongoing eye problems were susceptible to alcohol. He assured Miss Weaver that he was not an alcoholic as he did not drink during the day.

Miss Weaver, who was supporting James directly, also supported Sylvia Beach in preparing to publish *Ulysses* in England under the *Egoist Press* after the limited edition came out in Paris. Lists of potential subscribers were collected with literary figures, Yeats, Hemingway, Gide, Larbaud, lining up in support. George Bernard Shaw famously refused to subscribe, writing to Sylvia Beach on 10 October 1921; "*Ulysses is a revolting record of a disgusting civilisation; but it is a truthful one. In Ireland they try to make a cat cleanly by rubbing its nose in its own filth. Mr. Joyce has tried the same treatment on the human subject. I hope it may prove successful...if you imagine that any Irishman would pay 150 francs for a book, you little know my countrymen*[131]. Shaw was among many

---

[131] . Shakespeare & Company Paris 1959 p. 52.

who did not fully understand that Joyce was about finding "*a language, form and style that was new and inventive so that his work would not be answerable to any earlier tradition, set his masterpiece against any narrow idea of a nation. His nation of 1904 was made of different people in the same place*"[132]

James decided that *Ulysses* was to appear on his 40th birthday 2 February 1922. One copy came to him and another to Sylvia Beach's shop. The celebrations went on all day and James wanted to continue through the night until Nora directed him home. When later the Joyces were invited to a ballet on the special date of 16 June, Nora asked what was special about that date. She was often frank with their Irish friend Arthur Power as she was critical of the behaviour of the Parisian artistic class in which they then mixed constantly. When the family's finances became more secure, her thoughts turned to her family in Galway. She had not seen her mother for years and her father had died in July 1921. She decided to take her two children with her and travel to Galway. James was furious as Ireland in April 1922 was on the brink of civil war. James always feared the worst but Nora was determined to travel[133].

IRELAND 1916-1922

As we have seen when a revolution occurred in Dublin, James Joyce had become the beneficiary of badly needed official financial support from Britain. He therefore, unlike WB Yeats, remained mum on the events of the Easter Rising in 1916. The British military, under General Maxwell, quickly put down the Rising, executed sixteen men and interned hundreds in Britain. This was an over-reaction and

[132] . Lyons FSL, Culture and Anarchy in Ireland 1890-1939. Clarendon Press 1979.
[133] . Maddox Brenda p. 258.

gradually the Irish people, who at the beginning were generally against such a Rising, came to respect and revere those involved. As several of those involved were poets and teachers, it came to be known as the *'Poets' Revolution'*. WB Yeats himself was surprised how the Rising affected him and was soon immortalising the participants in a series of poems. Those interned later returned to Ireland as radicalised insurgents determined to continue the war against Britain. The British made a mistake in dubbing the Rising a *'Sinn Fein Rising'*. It was not, but soon the radicals, led by a teacher Eamon deValera, took control of the Sinn Fein organisation from its President and supporter of James Joyce, Arthur Griffith, and made it their own vehicle for challenging Britain's rule in Ireland. Sinn Fein won the post war General Election of 1918 in Ireland, refused to attend Westminster and set up their own Parliament, An Dail, in Dublin. An Anglo-Irish War followed from 1919-1921. Among those who lost their lives was Terence MacSweeney Lord Mayor of Cork. He died in Brixton Prison while being force-fed while on hunger strike. It was a *cause celebre*. James believed that there was a family connection with MacSweeney and reminiscent of his own battles with English bureaucracy in Zurich. He sent a suitably hostile poem to Stanislaus.

The right Heart in the Wrong Place

Of spinach and gammon

Bull's full to the crupper

White lice and black famine

Are the Mayor of Cork's supper

But the pride of old Ireland

Must be damnably humbled

If a Joyce is found cleaning

The boots of a Rumbold.

When a Truce was signed on 21 June 1921, Joyce's friend Valery
Larbaud was lecturing on *Ulysses*. Joyce remarked to him of the
coincidence. The Anglo-Irish Treaty was signed before Xmas by
Arthur Griffith[134], Michael Collins, Edward Duggan and Robert
Barton giving independence to twenty six out of thirty two counties of
Ireland. There followed in June 1922 a country-wide Civil War,
between those who accepted the Treaty and those who rejected it. It
was into this milieu that Nora Barnacle intended to visit her family in
Galway. James, who had an irrational fear of minor acts of violence,
was not able to change her mind. *Ulysses* was published and Miss
Weaver had solved their financial problems, so Nora decided to think
of what she wanted to do. With Georgio age seventeen and Lucia
aged fifteen, she arrived in London on 2 April 1922 and stayed
sightseeing for a few days. They all loved the place and Nora thought
that she might like to move there from Paris as James had several
good friends living in London. Nora's Uncle Michael Healy met them
in Dublin and entertained them there before they journeyed west to
Galway. They stayed in a boarding house at Nun's Island. The
children found Galway unsophisticated compared to Paris and Trieste
and refused to eat in Mrs Barnacle's terraced house. Nora loved
visiting her old haunts including the Presentation convent where she
had worked. As usual, James abandoned for the first time in five
years, was in a total panic back in Paris imaging the worst and writing
frequently. The one letter that survives reads:

---

[134] . Jordan Anthony J. *Arthur Griffith with James Joyce & WB Yeats- Liberating Ireland,* pp. 107-8.During the
protracted negotiations in London, Ezra Pound sought an interview with Arthur Griffith to discuss how
economic theory could cause war. As a result of this exchange Griffith features prominently in Pound's
masterpiece *The Cantos.*

8.30 a.m.

My darling, my love, my queen: I jump out of bed to send you this. Your wire is postmarked 18 hours later than your letter which I have just received. A cheque for your fur will follow in a few hours, and also money for yourself. If you wish to live there (as you ask me to send you two pounds a week) I will send that amount £8 and £4 for rent) on the first of every month. But you ask me if I would go to London with you. I would go anywhere in the world if I could be sure that I could be alone with your dear self without family and without friends. Either this must occur or we must part forever, though it will break my heart. Evidently it is impossible to describe to you the despair I have been in since you left. Yesterday I got a fainting fit in Miss Beach's shop and she had to run to get me some kind of a drug. Your image is always in my heart. How glad I am to hear that you are looking younger! O my dearest, if you would only turn to me even now and read that terrible book which has now broken the heart in my breast and take me to yourself alone to do with me what you will! I have only 10 minutes to write this so forgive me. Will write again before noon and also wire. These few words for the moment and my undying unhappy love.

Jim.

Regular gun fights were a feature of life in Galway between both sides in the emerging civil war. Nora and the children experienced it directly when gunmen rushed in to their boarding house to exchange fire with the enemy across the street. Nora decided that James was right. It was too dangerous and she packed and caught the next train out of Galway. As the train passed a military barracks in the city further gunfire sounded. In Dublin Nora told *Michael Healy* of their terror but he just laughed knowing the routine of gun fire in Galway.

Back in Paris James was certain that his family has faced assassination because of who they were. The Irish were trying to get at him again as usual. The Irish Civil War had come to James' rescue as the threat of Nora leaving him disappeared. This experience ended Nora's affection for her native place.

REACTIONS TO *ULYSSES*

Declan Kiberd writes accurately, *Ulysses would, like Joyce's earlier books, hold up a mirror to the colonial capital that was Dublin in 1904, but unlike them, it would also be a book of utopian epiphanies, hinting at a golden future which might be made over in terms of those utopian moments*[135]. The novel was set on 16 June 1904, *Bloomsday* forever more; it was the date on which Joyce first went for a walk with Nora Barnacle. Though Joyce had never returned to Ireland since 1912, he remained closer to it than most people who never left it. When he met visitors from Dublin he was full of detailed questions on people and places. Like so many emigrants and exiles he thought that time stood still back in the old country. Everything in Joyce's rooms in Paris spelt *Dublin*. There were pictures of old Dublin on the walls and even the design of the large rug, with which the floor was carpeted, portrayed the corkscrew course of the River Liffey[136]. He told Mrs Sheehy Skeffington that when he died '*Dublin*' would be found written on his heart[137].

When Joyce had been in Clongowes a priest had said that '*Ulysses is not a hero*'. *But to Joyce he was, on his own terms, for he had always admired this wily wanderer who had surmounted his difficulties with*

[135] . Kiberd Declan, Inventing Ireland p. 338.
[136] . Hone Joseph. WB Yeats 1942. P. 408.Joyce bought one of Jack B. Yeats' pictures of the Liffey, remarking to Jack that they both had the same method.
[137] . Sheehy p. 29.

determination and cunning: as stoically as Ulysses Joyce had condemned himself for years to such thankless tasks as keeping books, teaching and working in a bank rather than sell his talent, suffering from the continual snubs and frustrations of publishers but never losing sight of his ultimate purpose, constantly carrying this image of Dublin with him wherever he went, determined once and for all to break down the classical and romantic image which had dominated literature for so long[138].

Ulysses is a very complex novel and intentionally so. It was inspired by the story of the legendary Greek king of Ithaca and hero of Homer's *Odyssey*, notable for his cunning. His many adventures during his voyage home from the Trojan War included encounters with the Cyclops Polyphemus, the cannibalistic Laestrygones, the enchantress Circe and the goddess Calypso, with whom he lived for eight years. Having reached Ithaca, he was reunited with his faithful wife Penelope after killing her suitors with the help of his son Telemachus.

The action in Joyce's *Ulysses* centres on three main characters over twenty fours hours; Leopold Bloom, a salesman of advertisements who is Jewish by ancestry, Christian by baptism, Irish by birth, sceptical by reflection, and kindly by nature. His wife Molly is an attractive, streetwise, broadminded and talented singer. Stephen Dedalus, a teacher, writer and eloquent literary theorist who had been the central character in Portrait of the Artist as a Young Man[139]. It is divided into many sections, each with its own name in reference to the epic journey of Ulysses;

Episodes of '*Ulysses*': pagination as per Wordsworth 2010.
[Book I – The Telemachiad – episodes 1-3]

---

[138] . O'Connor Ulick Ed. *The Joyce we knew* , Power Arthur p. 96.
[139] . Watts Cedric, Introduction to *Ulysses*, Wordworth 2010, p. xviii

18 – Penelope – "Yes because he never did a thing like that before"
p. 664

Ulysses was praised by many famous literary figures like TS Eliot,
Ezra Pound, WB Yeats, Ernest Hemingway, Gertrude Stein [though
jealous that he never sought to meet her though they lived quite close
in Paris]. Some disputed its greatness. One who did was Edmund
Gosse who had assisted Joyce and WB Yeats to get State pensions.
Gosse wrote to Louis Gillet of the, *"worthlessness and impudence of
his writings. I have a difficulty in describing in writing, the character
of Mr. Joyce's notoriety. It is partly political; it is partly a perfectly
cynical appeal to sheer indecency. He is a literary charlatan of the
extremist order. It is an anarchical production, infamous in taste, in
style, in everything. Mr. Joyce is unable to publish or sell his books
in England, on account of their obscenity. He therefore issues a
'private' edition in Paris, and charges a huge price for each copy. He
is a sort of Marquis de Sade, but does not write so well. He is the
perfect type of the Irish fumiste, a hater of England, more than
suspected of partiality for Germany, where he lived before the war
(and at Zurich during the war). There are no English critics of weight
or judgement who consider Mr. Joyce as an author of any
importance…He is not as I say, without talent, but he has prostituted
it to the most vulgar uses"[140]*. Virginia Woolf thought the book
*underbred…the book of a self-taught working man, a queasy
undergraduate scratching his pimples[141]*.

The Irish writer George Moore said, *"Joyce, Joyce, why he's
nobody—from the Dublin docks; no family no breeding. Ulysses is
hopeless. That's not art, it's like trying to copy the London
directory"[142]*. Joyce defended this aspect of the book by claiming that

---

[140] . Gillet Louis, *Claybook for James Joyce*, p. 31-2

[141] . Woolfe Virginia, *A Writers Diary* p. 47 & 49.

[142]. George Moore, *Intimate Portraits* Barrett Clarke 1951 p. 110.

he was giving such a complete picture of Dublin that it could be reconstructed from the book.

Joyce's family in Dublin were scandalised by the book with his father remarking, *"He's a nice sort of blackguard"*. Stanislaus still in Trieste told James that *"Dublin is spread out before the reader"* but while liking some episodes he disliked others. When Lady Gregory asked permission to quote from a letter in the book Joyce refused, writing bitterly that since he had written to her twenty years ago; *"no mention of me or of my struggles or of my writings has been made publicly by any person connected with it*[143]. Nora thought it obscene though recognising much of the little she ever read of it.

In 1920 Joyce had described Ulysses as the epic of two races (Israel and Ireland) with a history of dispersal, persecution, survival and revival. By placing an endlessly complex and deeply human Jewish figure at the centre of his novel, he was also engaging in a political act, a challenge to Europe's hostile attitude towards the Jews. While Joyce did know Jews in Dublin he came to know the far more prominent and varied Jewish community of Trieste and Paris[144].

Declan Kiberd writes, *"Like Yeats, Joyce presented himself as a modern Homer, a type of the epic narrator even in his reluctance to begin…Like all epics, his would only be given its full expression in the act of being read aloud"*[145].

When Random House published it in 1934 they explained it in an advertisement; *for those who are already engrossed in the reading of Ulysses as well as those who hesitate to begin it because they fear that it is obscure, the publisher offers this simple clue to what the critical fuss is all about. Ulysses is no harder to 'understand' that any other great classic. It is essentially a story and can be enjoyed as*

---

[143] . Lady Gregory, *Selected Letters* 1922 p. 290.

[144] . McCourt p. 217.

[145] . Kiberd Declan, *Inventing Ireland* Vintage 1996 p. 355.

such. Bloom is everyman and goes on his journey through Dublin, the episodes of Ulysses present modern versions of Odysseus' adventures. Bloom seems like an ordinary man from the outside and his conversations are unremarkable. But his inner life is very rich. We build up a picture of an ordinary, humane, decent man, insulted and ridiculed by almost everyone. Most of the characters are male and there is an unusual preoccupation with bodily functions that have given it a reputation of a 'dirty' book[146].

In a lecture, already referred to in the Introduction, at the National Library Ireland in the summer of 2016, Luke Gibbons of Maynooth University saw *Ulysses* as a '*performance*' much like the Easter Rising: they did not represent a city (or country) that was already in place, but helped to transform it, and give it a new modern identity. 1904 and 1916 were not comprised of static events but continued on in time and having an ongoing relevance to each age. The ongoing worldwide interest in *Ulysses,* notwithstanding its intense local address, appears to corroborate this interpretation, and the 1916 Rising was no less international in its scope.

President Michael D Higgins, speaking to the American Irish Historical Society in New York in 2012 said, *James Joyce drew on so much of the memory baggage of his people, yet he did not surrender it to what he inherited as the form of the novel. After his early stories, he did not adhere to the craft of imitation that was available to him in the prevailing genre of social realism. In his great novel Ulysses, he brought something entirely new into the world*[147].

---

[146] . Groden Michael, *the Complete Simplicity of James Joyce* p. 107 & 116, in *James Joyce* by Sean Latham.

[147] . Higgins Michael D. *When Ideas Matter*, Head of Zeus U. 2016.p. 89.

Perhaps one of the more exciting things that happened to James in connection with the book was a visit from a Minister in the new Irish Government. Desmond Fitzgerald, father of Taoiseach Garrett Fitzgerald[148], was a London-born poet who had been a member of the *Imagist* group of poets with Ezra Pound. He became an Irish nationalist  who participated in the Easter Rising and was interned along with Arthur Griffith in Gloucester Jail. Fitzgerald was then Minster of External Affairs. He told Joyce that he intended to have Joyce nominated for the Nobel Prize for Literature. Jim wrote Stanislaus on 3/2/1922, *"the Dail Eireann minister of propaganda called on me and wished to know if I intended to return to Ireland – to which I returned an evasive answer. He is proposing me, it seems, for the Nobel prize in his capacity of cabinet Minister as soon as the Treaty is ratified at Westminster, though not in the name of his cabinet. I will take on a small bet that if he does not change his mind when he sees the complete text he will lose his portfolio while I have not the faintest chance of being awarded the prize".* Joyce was never nominated for the Nobel Literature Prize. Marie Heaney confirmed this to me after she and Seamus Heaney had specifically asked this question when they were in Sweden for Seamus' prize giving in 2005[149]. Many people today are surprised by this omission but it has happened to a wide variety of famous writers such as Zola, Ibsen, Twain, Tolstoy, Proust, Woolf, Auden. Joyce had died before modernist writers began to be favoured by the Nobel Prize Committee. It is ironic that it was WB Yeats, after being nominated unsuccessfully several times previously for the Nobel Prize, who would be the person to win it in 1923.

---

[148] . Garrett FitzGerald was Taoiseach from 1981-1987

[149] . That conversation took place atop the Railway Bridge to the rear of Merrion Road Church Dublin 4.

As James' fame grew so did his financial stability. Nora suggested a family trip to Ireland but James refused.

Chapter 12.

ARTHUR GRIFFITH HONOURED IN '*ULYSSES*'

Arthur Griffith with his two children at his home in Clontarf

The publication of *Ulysses* had coincided with the coming into being of the new Irish State with Arthur Griffith as President. Richard Ellmann writes that *"The prominence of Griffith in the book seemed an anticipation of his assumption of the presidency"*[150]. Ellmann adds,*"For a moment it seemed that the two events were allied, that Ireland would be a nation once again in terms of both spiritual and political emancipation. But Griffith died after only a few months in power, and Joyce had second thoughts"*[151]. It is an ironic fact that as Arthur Griffith, the sober editor and involuntary politician, who gave his life in the service of his country, has been largely forgotten in

---

[150] Ellmann p. 792 note 44.
[151] . Ellmann p. 533.

Ireland, while his main prospect for immortality lies in James Joyce's *Ulysses*. A close inspection of the book reveals Griffith's presence throughout, even in Molly Bloom's soliloquy. In *Ulysses* Joyce acknowledges the political importance of Griffith by making many references to him, alone of the politicians of his day, and he called attention to the ultimately political direction of his own work by having Irish Stephen, at the end of the brothel scene, beaten up by a British soldier, whom he describes as '*The Uninvited*'"[152].

D.R Lysaght O'Connor wrote of *Ulysses* in 2004," *the only green shoots of which the author of Ulysses approves of is the United Irishman through which Arthur Griffith was preparing the way for Sinn Fein. Joyce began planning his novel in 1907 when matters were becoming more interesting. And he wrote it between 1914 and 1922when the green shoots had become sturdy plants. Now it is certainly possible to argue that the novel is anti-political. Against this, as if lighting the way forward, there stands the isolated figure of Leopold Bloom, and, behind him, the shadow of Arthur Griffith,unable to do more than point the future, because in 1904, that was all they could do*"[153].

Richard Ellmann writes that, *"Ulysses creates new Irishmen to live in Griffith's new state"*. Among the references to Griffith in Ulysses is that, "*John Wyse said it was* Bloom *gave the idea for Sinn Fein to Griffith to put in his paper*". The several references to Griffith and Sinn Fein in *Ulysses* demonstrate that Joyce had an intimate and detailed knowledge of Griffith and what he was about. This is in no way surprising as Joyce's father John, was an avid participant in many of those events, which formed the backdrop to Joyce's own youth. The central character of the novel, the Jew Leopold Bloom, wanders about Dublin. I give below a example of the extracts featuring Griffith. The passage that most appeals to me concerns the whimsical proposition that if you rose before sunrise and kept

---

[152] . Lysaght O'Connorr, *Ulysses As a Political novel, Social Democracy.* 17/6/2004.
[153] . Ibid.

 walking fast before the sun actually rose, you would never grow old. As Leopold Bloom enters the story in the fourth scene, he is letting himself out of his house quietly early in the morning so as not to disturb his wife Molly:

1. *Calypso* Chapter 4.

"On the doorstep he felt in his hip pocket for the latchkey. Not there. In the trousers I left off. Must get it. No use disturbing her. He pulled the halldoor too after him very quietly. Looked shut. All right till I come back anyhow.
He crossed to the bright side, avoiding the loose cellarflap of number seventyfive. The sun was nearing the steeple of George's church. Be a warm day I fancy. Boland's breadvan delivering with trays our daily... Makes you feel young. Somewhere in the east: early morning:

set off at dawn, travel round in front of the sun, steal a day's march on him. Keep it up for ever never grow a day older technically... Probably not a bit like it really. Kind of stuff you read: in the track of the sun. Sunburst on the titlepage. He smiled, pleasing himself. What Arthur Griffith said about the headpiece over the Freeman leader: a homerule sun rising up in the northwest from the laneway behind the bank of Ireland. He prolonged his pleased smile. Ikey touch that:homerule sun rising up in the northwest"[154]

In the **Proteus** Episode Joyce refers to the visit to Ireland of Queen Victoria in 1900 to help encourage Irishmen to enlist in the British army for the Boer War. Maud Gonne, whom Griffith loved, and her French lover Lucien Millevoye, the father of her first two children, also feature. Stephen Dedalus setting off from Mr Deasy's school in Dalkey has entered Sandymount Strand from Leahy's Terrace.

"There was a fellow I knew once in Barcelona, queer fellow, used to call it his postprandial. Well: slainte! ... Of Ireland, the Dalcassians,

[154] . Joyce *Ulysses* Wordsworth 2010. Calypso. p. 50

of hopes, conspiracies, of Arthur Griffith now. To yoke me as his yokefellow, our crimes our common cause. You're your father's son. I know the voice. His fustian shirt, sanguineflowered, trembles its Spanish tassels at his secrets. M. Drumont, famous journalist, Drumont, know what he called queen Victoria? Old hag with the yellow teeth. Vieille ogresse with the dents jaunes. Maud Gonne, beautiful woman, La Patrie, M. Millevoye... "[155].

In a passage dealing with the political ideas of the day, Joyce writes:*You must have a certain fascination: Parnell. Arthur Griffith is a square-headed fellow but he has no go in him for the mob. Or gas about our lovely land. Gammon and spinach. Dublin Bakery's company tearoom. Debating societies. That republicanism is the bestForm of government. That the language question should take precedence of the economic question*[156].

In the **Clycops** chapter set in a Little Britain St pub, Joyce deals with Griffith's '*Resurrection of Hungary*'. The *Citizen* is apparently based on Michael Cusack, founder of the GAA. '*Shanganagh*' was one of the pen names Griffith used in the *United Irishman*.

-- *Is that by Griffith? says John Wyse.*

-- *No, says the citizen. It's not signed Shanganagh. It's only initialled: P.*

-- *And a very good initial too, says Joe.*

-- *That's how it's worked, says the citizen. Trade follows the flag.*

-- *Well, says J. J., if they're any worse than those Belgians in the Congo Free State they must be bad. Did you read that report by a man what's this his name is?*

-- *Casement, says the citizen. He's an Irishman.*

---

[155] . ibid p. 39. Proteus
[156] . p. 145.Lestrygonians.

-- Yes, that's the man, says J. J. Raping the women and girls and flogging the natives on the belly to squeeze all the red rubber they can out of them...

So anyhow when I got back they were at it dingdong, John Wyse saying it was Bloom gave the idea for Sinn Fein to Griffith to put in his paper all kinds of jerrymandering, packed juries and swindling the taxes off of the Government and appointing consuls all over the world to walk about selling Irish industries. Robbing Peter to pay Paul. Gob, that puts the bloody kybosh on it if old sloppy eyes is mucking up the show. Give us a bloody chance. God save Ireland from the likes of that bloody mouseabout. Mr Bloom with his argol bargol.

- Well, it's a fact, says John Wyse. And there's the man now that'll tell you about it, Martin Cunningham.

So in comes Martin asking where was Bloom.

-- Isn't that a fact, says John Wyse, what I was telling the citizen about Bloom and the Sinn Fein?

-- That's so, says Martin. Or so they allege.

-- Who made those allegations? says Alf.

- He's a perverted jew, says Martin, from a place in Hungary and it was he drew up all the plans according to the Hungarian system. We know that in the castle.

-- Isn't he a cousin of Bloom the dentist? says Jack Power[157].

When Joyce lists famous Irish leaders at odds with each other, Griffith is included; "*Wolfe Tone against Henry Grattan, Smith O'Brien against Daniel O'Connell, Michael Davitt against Isaac Butt, Justin McCarthy against Parnell, Arthur Griffith against John Redmond...*"[158].

[157]. ibid p. 302-3. Cyclops
[158] Ibid. P. 581. Ithaca.

In the most wonderfully erotic soliloquy in English literature, in which Molly Bloom ends *Ulysses,* Griffith features. Molly, the singer, talks about how she got work through a certain man until the Jesuits discovered that he was a Freemason " *and he was going about with some of them sinner Fein lately or whatever they call themselves talking his usual trash and nonsense he says that little man he showed me without the neck is very intelligent the coming man Griffith is he*

well he doesn't look it that's all I can say still it must have been him he knew there was a boycott I hate the mention of politics...."[159].

[159]. ibid p. 650. Penople

Chapter 13.

LIVING THE GOODLIFE IN PARIS

WB YEATS WINS NOBEL PRIZE

Cedric Watts has written, *Thanks to generous patronage, the Joyce's could enjoy an affluent lifestyle in Paris in the 1930's entertaining guests lavishly, dining at expensive restaurants, and travelling abroad for holidays*[160].

When James' father heard of his son's financial good fortune he wrote looking for some money. James replied telling John how he was sorely put to make ends meet and telling him that John's pension of £150 per annum was better off than himself. John lived out his final years living *with a family where he had board and room for around twenty five or thirty shillings a week with people who knew nothing of the great times when he was a sport among Dublin sports, when his tenor notes were praised by an admired singer, and when there were people who knew he had hunted over every field in County Cork*[161]

In 1923 Miss Weaver inherited around £12,000 and granted it to James. This could have made him independent financially for the rest of his life if he had been able to manage it, but of course he was not. The family moved into the Grand hotel for a year while searching for a permanent place of their own. James' eye operations, his drinking and Nora's disgust continued without end. Despite this James began Finnegan's Wake in 1923 with Nora *as Anna Livia Plurabelle*. He

---

[160] . Watt Cedric, Ulysses Introduction, Wordsworth Classics 2010, p. XI
[161] . Colm Mary & Padraig. P. 201.

was forced to get her to help with note taking. She added "To *day 16 June 1924 twenty years after. Will anybody remember this day*[162]."
Despite the uproar caused by the content of his writings James and Nora were traditionalists in many ways. They were shattered to discover that Georgio aged 20 was having an affair with their friend Helen Fleischman aged 31 and the mother of a boy[163]. This made them even more vigilant about Lucia, who was already appearing to be '*different*' to their friends.

It was only natural that Desmond Fitzgerald Minister for Information and poet would be an admirer of Joyce and wish to '*capture*' him for the new State, as John O'Leary had earlier '*captured*' Yeats for Ireland. Though invited to return to Ireland in March 1922 by Fitzgerald, Joyce replied "*Not for the present*". He was fearful of his reception and the outbreak of civil war. As a man fearful of violence he felt that after the publication of his three books, he might have made enemies in Ireland. He might suffer the same fate as Parnell had, after his return after the O'Shea divorce case, when someone threw quick lime thrown into Parnell's eyes. As Joyce's eyesight was problematical, this would be a nightmare for him. Extracts of *Ulysses* had been published earlier and the novel had gained a reputation of notoriety and scandal in Ireland.

---

[162] . Maddox Brenda p. 57.
[163] . ibid p. 301.

Mr & Mrs WB Yeats in Stockholm

In the event, as we have seen, the new State received a mark of international recognition and honour when WB Yeats was awarded the Nobel Prize for Literature in 1923.

Two Irishmen had been nominated in 1922, Darrell Figgis nominated by Thomas B. Rudmore-Brown and WB Yeats by the Nobel Committee. Yeats' earliest nomination came in 1902 from William Lecky. In 1914 George Plunkett nominated Yeats and he was nominated again in 1915 by Per Hallstrom, a member of the Swedish Academy. In 1921 Yeats received a nomination from Erik Axel Karlfeldt, a poet and member of the Swedish Academy. The Committee nominated Yeats again in 1923, when he was finally successful[164].

The money was very welcome, giving the poet financial independence. But he was astute enough to recognise its wider meaning as he announced, *"I consider that this honour has come to me less as an individual than as a representative of Irish literature, it is part of Europe's welcome to the Free State"*. His Swedish Academy lecture was titled *'The Irish Dramatic Movement'*. Yeats later published a book, *The Bounty of Sweden*, dealing with the Irish renaissance with himself, Lady Gregory and JM Synge at the centre, as if they came out of a vacuum. He wrote in a passage that Griffith and Joyce would have probably agreed, *"The modern literature of Ireland, and indeed all that stir of thought which prepared for the Anglo-Irish war, began when Parnell fell from power in 1891. A disillusioned and embittered Ireland turned from parliamentary politics; an event was conceived; and the race began, as I think, to be troubled by that event's long gestation"*. Yeats's struggles with Arthur Griffith and the Griffithites was dealt with thus, ' *Every political party had the same desire to substitute for life, which never does the*

---

[164] . Details from a paper read by the author at the 2016 Annual Yeats Birthday Commemoration he organises at Sandymount Green.

same thing twice, a bundle of reliable principles and assertions... It is too soon yet to say what will come to us from the melodrama and tragedy of the last four years "[165].

WG Fallon recalled that when in Paris to see an international rugby match he met Joyce afterwards and was surprised that Joyce had also been at the game. Joyce said, *"I had to go to see the boys in green jerseys"*. When Fallon was again in Paris in 1931 for a match Joyce phoned him and had two tickets for the game. They met afterwards and Joyce admitted that his eyes were not strong enough for him to identify *'our team'*. He knew the names of each player and their respective clubs. He also said how he always attended the France v Ireland games when he was in Paris. I noticed that he still spoke with a good class Dublin accent[166].

YEATS & *ULYSSES*

WB Yeats at first thought it a *"mad book"* after reading sections in the *Little Review* in 1918. But he quickly came on board writing, *"It is an entirely new thing...He has certainly surpassed in intensity any novelist of our time*[167]. Yeats praised the book saying, *"It has our Irish cruelty and also our kind of strength...A cruel playful mind like a great soft tiger cat...I will have to hide him from our politicians, who are not yet ready for his doctrine"*[168]. Though he tried, Yeats did not finish reading *Ulysses*[169].

The Yeatses, the Pounds and the Joyces met for dinner in Paris in late 1922. Joyce thought that Yeats had *"that touch of pugnacity of manner"* that he had as a young man. After this Yeats began to praise the book publicly.

[165] . Yeats WB, *the Bounty of Sweden,* Irish University Press, 1925.
[166] . O'Connor Ulick Ed, *The Joyce We Knew.*
[167] . Yeats WB, *Letters,* p. 651 to John Quinn July 1918.
[168] .Hone Joseph, *WB Yeats 1865-1938* MacMillan 1942. P. 347-8.
[169] . ibid p. 678. to Olivia Shakespeare 8/3/1922.

In June 1923 Yeats wrote to Joyce, *"Have you any wish to revisit Dublin? If so will you spend a few days with us? If you will come soon as we may be flitting to Galway in a couple of weeks. My wife and I have a great admiration for your work and there are many people here who share our admiration. Perhaps you would like to meet some of them – a new literary generation*[170].

Yeats sought an official invitation for Joyce to the Government approved Tailtean Games in 1924, but the committee rejected his request. Yeats then issued a personal invitation to Joyce to attend, but he declined.

At a meeting in Trinity College Dublin Yeats made his most public defence of the novel, *"James Joyce was certainly as voluminous as Johnston's dictionary and as foul as Rabelais. But he was the only Irishman who had the intensity of the great novelist"*[171].

In 1925 the Joyces finally moved into an unfurnished rented apartment. Their traditional decorations and design embarrassed their *avant garde* friends who expected examples of modern art rather than pictures of their own family as was the way they might have decorated a home in Dublin. As James' Aunt Josephine lay dying he wrote to her on 2 November 1924, *"You attached me to you in youth by so many acts of kindness, by so much help and advice and sympathy, especially after my mother's death, that it seems to me as if your thought of me now is one of reproach...but if I am estranged in that I am still attached to you by many bonds of gratitude and affection and out of respect as well.* Josephine was disaffected by *Ulysses* and by Nora not visiting her during her visit to Dublin in 1922.

The fact that the Joyces now had their own home encouraged their relatives to visit, though they had to be put up in local

---

[170] . Yeats WB *Letters*
[171] . *Irish Times* 9/11/1923

accommodation. Michael Healy came from Galway. Other friends came from Ireland. The Joyces were hosts to local literati as well as their own friends. Nora always kept her house immaculately. Though some continued to be critical of her as *'unworthy'* of such a great writer, most recognised her natural qualities and the fact that James could not live without her. A family crisis occurred in 1926 when Eileen Joyce's husband, Frank Schaurek, shot himself.

In April 1928 James was godfather to Ford Maddox's daughter in a Catholic ceremony. He said he did it *'as an act of kindness' i.e. removing the devil from a baby girl.*

SAMUEL BECKETT

In 1928 a very good Parisian friend of the Joyce's Tom McGreevy introduced the 23 year old Samuel Beckett to the family[172]. Beckett was happy to get the opportunity to assist Joyce on a regular basis, becoming a daily visitor to the family flat. He enjoyed Nora's company and almost became a part of the family. By 1930 Lucia had developed a crush on Beckett and when this was not reciprocated it lead to a temporary family rupture with Beckett who was very upset by the outcome. Lucia was very distressed as her mental stability deteriorated[173]. This was to be a continuing cross James had to bear for his whole life.

George Moore wrote from London to James in September 1929 about Ulysses, *"Dear Mr Joyce, When we look back upon our lives, our lives seem fateful. I never understood why I avoided reading Ulysses for I was curious to read it, and when I was in the Nursing Home somebody sent me the present of a reading desk! I am reading Ulysses and if you were here for a longer time and could dine with me, we would talk about the French, which I think wilfully exaggerated in places.*

---

[172] . Maddox Brenda p. 322.
[173] . Maddox Brenda pp. 322-337.

Thank you for sending the book.

George Moore   *Samuel Beckett*   *Tom McGreevy*

CHAPTER 14.

MARRIAGE

John Francis Byrne visited the Joyce's in 1927. It was the first time he had seen Nora since 1904. He encountered a most happy home where James was finishing his *Work in Progress* which was being published monthly in *Transition*. James persuaded his guest to stay longer than planned and wrote to Mrs Byrne: *I am very glad to meet my old friend Byrne after so many years and it is most kind of you to allow him to stay a few days. I hope you will not be annoyed if we press him to stay over the weekend as the weather is very fine and he ought to see a number of things here before he leaves. The change too will do him good. He will go back on Monday or Tuesday unless you wish him to return earlier.*

Byrne went on a shopping trip with Nora one day. She confided in him that she would like to be married to James. He agreed to raise the subject with James who assented[174].

28 Campden Grove Kensington, London

---

[174] . Byrne JF. pp. 149-150

James and Nora married on 4 July 1931, the date of his father's birthday, in a London Registry Office. The register records; *James Augustine Joyce, aged 49, Bachelor, Independent means married Nora Joseph Barnacle, Spinster, aged 47, each then residing at 28B Campden Grove, London W.8. on 4th July 1931. Father of man, John Stanislaus Joyce, Government Clerk, (Pensioned). Father of woman, Thomas Barnacle, decd. Baker.* James told his solicitor that he could not explain very clearly why he wished his son and grandson to bear his name but he did[175]. James did not want the press to find out about his marriage as he was already supposed to have married in 1904 and gave just one day's notice. But a reporter noticed it listed on the Kensington Registry Office schedule. Newspaper reporters laid siege to their house in London. His solicitor, Fred Munro, advised him to tell the truth and to say that the marriage was for 'domestic reasons' but that he used the term 'testamentary reasons'. James insisted that there was a marriage in 1904 in Austria and was then asked to explain why Nora had been described as '*Spinster*' on the Register?[176] . A disapproving article appeared in the American *Catholic World* newspaper written by Judge Michael Lennon of Dublin who had earlier met Joyce in Paris. He wrote of Nora as a waitress in Dublin whom Joyce "*did not grant the protection of even a civil marriage, protesting at the time that he would have no church ceremony or priest's work over his alliance, but that he would deal fairly by the girl, a promise which he has kept. She must have been strangely infatuated with him to enter into such a partnership. She had borne him a girl and a boy, each of whom is now over twenty years of age...*"[177]. In 1937 Joyce wrote to Constantine Curran saying that he

[175] . Irish Times 1 August 2014.
[176] . Irish Times report 1/8/2014 on letters acquired by National Library Ireland
[177] . Michael Lennon *Catholic World*, March 1931.

would not return to Ireland as the map of his countrymen was clearly marked '*Hic sunt Lennones*'.

The couple received an invitation from Padraig Colum and his wife to visit Dublin. Joyce replied;" *as regards your kind Dublin offer I cannot make up my mind to cross the second channel. My sight is too weak. I have not enough funds. I have not a friend in Dublin on whom I could rely...And too much publicity was given that Kensington ceremony*". A sister of Nora's Kathleen visited them in London and was told by Nora that the one thing she hated about life in Paris was going out to dinner and sitting with artists till 01.00 in the morning and being bored stiff. When they visited Madame Tussaud's Waxworks Kathleen told James that she wanted to see him among the exhibits. During a visit to Paris in 1931 James remarked to Padraig Colum, *Isn't it extraordinary that none of my family read anything I write*"[178].

In August 1932 James received a letter form CG Jung.
Dear Sir,
Your Ulysses has presented the world such an upsetting psychologic problem that repeatedly I have been called in as a supposed authority on psychological matters.
Ulysses proved to be an exceedingly hard nut and it has forced my mind not only to most unusual efforts but also to a rather extravagant peregrination. Your book as a whole has given me no end of trouble and I was brooding over it for three years until I succeeded in pulling myself into it. But I must tell you that I am profoundly grateful to yourself as to your gigantic enterprise opus, because I learned a great deal from it. I shall probably be never quite sure whether I did enjoy it, because it meant too much grinding of nerves and grey matter. I also don't know whether you will enjoy what I have written about Ulysses because I couldn't help telling the world how much I was

---

[178] . Colum Mary, p. 198.

bored, how I grumbled, how I cursed, and how I admired...I suppose the devil's grandmother knows so much about the real psychology of a woman. I didn't. Well I just try to recommend my little essay to you[179].

James was not amused by what Jung wrote about his book and wrote: *"He seems to have read it from first to last without a smile. The only thing to do in such a case is to change one's drink".*

Yeats wrote again to Joyce to Dublin in 1932 inviting him to become a member of an Academy of Letters.

Riversdale, Willbrook, Rathfarnham, Dublin.
September 2 1932

My dear Joyce,

Bernard Shaw and I are busy founding an Academy of Irish Letters, we are nominating the first members, twenty five, who have done creative work with Ireland as the subject matter...Of course the first name that seemed essential both to Shaw and myself was your own...All the writers here who are likely to form our Council are students of your work.

Yours sincerely

W B Yeats

George Moore ignored the invitation and refusals came from Douglas Hyde, Stephen McKenna and James Joyce. Joyce's refusal was the chief disappointment. Despite all that Yeats had done for him, Joyce declined the request, writing on 5 October.

Hotel Metropole Nice

---

[179] . Ein Monologue September 1932

Dear Yeats,

> *Many thanks for your letter and the kind words you use. It is now thirty years since you first held out to me your helping hand...I hope that the Academy of Letters which you both are founding [GBS] will have the success it aims at. My case, however, being as it was and probably will be, I see no reason why my name should have arisen at all in connection with such an academy: and I feel quite clearly that I have no right whatsoever to nominate myself as a member of it...* "[180].

In a series of letters to various members of the Joyce family James made some interesting comments: On being contacted about purchasing tickets for the Irish Hospital Sweepstakes in 1934 he responded, *"No, I am not interested in the Irish Sweepstake tickets. The only decent people I ever saw at a race meeting were the horses."* He added a memory from home, *"Mr. Guckian, used to say Pappie had the best tenor voice in Ireland in his time. We used to have merry evenings in our house, used we not?* He added, *"In my first public concert I too was left in the lurch. The pianist, that is the lady pianist, had gone away right in the middle of the concert. I sang 'Down By the Sally Gardens' and I received exactly ten dollars or two guineas like you. Ballynure Ballad, Bally means city in the province of Ulster, today Northern Ireland or the Six counties. A mixed breed; Irish, English, and may be Scottish in origin. Tough, tenacious, hard drinkers and hard workers, very hostile to the Pope and all his pomps and works. The 5th day of November is Guy Fawkes Day... In my day the Lord Mayor was elected by the members of the Corporation to whom he owed money so that they could get a garnisher order on his salary...What could any burglar hope to get by entering the house of any member of the Joyce family? I am short of cash this weekend but will win £5 more .P.S. I didn't know the Irish Paddies celebrate their*

---

[180] . Hone Joseph, *WB Yeats* 1942 p. 426-7.

onomastico (Saints day). I mean Patrick Schaurk)...Some days ago I had to renew my passport. The clerk told me that he had orders to send people like me to the Irish Legation. I insisted and got another. ..I hope the Brighton of Ireland is behaving better [Bray]*...".*

CJ Jung

In 1936 Joyce was told that Yeats had remarked in 1924, *"Isn't it remarkable that Joyce, who hasn't been in Dublin since he was a young man, writes only about Dublin?"* Yeats summarised Joyce as, *"the son of a small Parnellite organiser, had begun to write in 1902 though not yet to publish; he was an exile, at first in Zurich, then in Paris, in flight from the objects of his hatred, bearing in mind always in minute detail, even to the names over the shops, the Dublin that he hated but would not forget".*

On an American tour in 1936-7 Yeats was asked about censorship in the new Ireland. On Joyce he said, *"Well the Irish propagandists drove James Joyce from Ireland. I think he came to hate the illusory Ireland and so he went into exile. That was thirty years ago. Since then he has spent his time writing, studying, a few days or weeks at the end of the nineteenth century in Ireland, and writing about them from his own inner consciousness. And no man can say now whether it is from hate or love that he writes*"[181].

In 1936 Stanislaus contacted James to say that he was to be expelled from Italy to Switzerland where James met him.

A FALLING-OUT WITH SYLVIA BEACH

& HARRIET WEAVER

In 1932 Harriet Weaver suggested to Joyce that he was spending his capital rather freely and should try to live on his income. He responded impatiently and Harriet was remorseful and apologised in person.

After some persuasion Sylvia Beach handed over her world rights in *Ulysses* for a small percentage of royalty income following Joyce's insistence. James wrote to Harriet Weaver, *Possibly the fault is mine. I, my eye, my needs and my troublesome books are always there.* Joyce's constant badgering for cash led to a falling-out between them. When Andre Gide commented that Joyce's courage in carrying his literary experiments to the limit, indifferent to success or money, had something saintly about it, Beach's partner, Adrienne Monnier, had enough. She wrote to Joyce; *What Gide doesn't know is that you are, on the contrary, very concerned about success and you wish others also to go to the limit; you lead by rough stages to some Dublingrad or other place, which they're not interested in, or rather, you try to lead them. My personal opinion is that you know perfectly well what you are doing in literature, and that you are quite right to do it, especially if it entertains you; life isn't so funny at any cost with your*

---

[181] . *Boston Evening* transcript 9/12/1932

new work. I won't say that you can't make any, everything is possible, but it is most unlikely. Times are hard and the worst isn't over. We're travelling now third class and soon we'll be riding the rods.
Give my best regards to Mrs Joyce and Lucia, and be assured, dear Mr. Joyce, of my very great and faithful admiration.

Adrienne Monnier[182].

Monnier was referring to the *Great Depression* and the probability that *Work in Progress* would not bring in much money. The Depression forced many Americans to leave Paris and return home as investment returns plummeted. One of the last to remain as a drinking companion for Joyce was Ernest Hemingway until he departed to report on the Spanish Civil War in 1936.

Paul Leon was a Russian Jewish scholar, an admirer of Joyce's writings who became a close friend together with his wife Lucie. They began to play a large role in both James' and Nora's lives. In April James wrote to Harriet Weaver, "*Although I have the faithful support of my wife and Leon's loyal friendship, to say nothing of your own patience and sympathy, there are moments and hours, when I have nothing in my heart but rage and despair, a blind man's rage and despair. Paris is like a haughty ruin, or a decaying reveller...Perhaps Ireland or the U.S. are the safest places*"[183]. Leon would later devote himself to the rescue of Joyce's papers sorting and stuffing them into large brown envelopes before handing them over to the Irish ambassador, Count O'Kelly[184].

FINNEGAN'S WAKE

James wrote to Stanislaus in April 1939 that his book *Finnegan's Wake* would be published on 4 May. He thought it expensive at 25 shillings. James told *Signora Maria Nebbia* [Larbard's friend] that the

---

[182] . Ellmann Richard, *James Joyce*, p. 651.

[183] . Price Stanley, p. 247.

[184] . Cronin Anthony Samuel Beckett the Last Modernist, Flamingo 1997. p. 320.

book would be published in America and London on St Monica's Day. He pondered whether it was wise for him to have spent 18 years of his life *"completing that monster of a book. But what can one do? One is born that way. Yet, by God, I have had enough. And that's that"*. The Sunday Times refused to review it as *"irrelevant to literature"*. Oliver Gogarty wrote in the Observer, *"In some places the reading sounds like the chatter during the lunch interval in a Berlitz School. This is the most colossal leg-pull in literature"*[185]. Stanislaus, who continued to have a difficult life, had often urged James to desist from writing that book. He regarded it as the result of all the praise James had received and wished him to write something of greater worth. A short extract reads:

> *He dug in and dug out by the skill of his tilth for himself and all belonging to him and he sweated is crew beneath his auspice for the living and he urned his dread, that dragon volant, and he made louse for us and delivered us to boll weevils amain, that mighty liberator, Unfru-Chikda-Uru-Wukru and begad he did, our ancestor most worshipful, till he thought of a better one in his windower's house with that blushmantle upon him from ears-end to earsend. And would again could whispring grassies wake him and may again when the fiery bird disembers. And will again if so be sooth by elder to his youngers shall be said. Have you whines for my wedding, did you bring bride and bedding, will you whoop for my deading is a? Wake? Usgueadbaugham!*
> *Anam muck an dhoul! Did ye drink me doornail?*

The Guardian published a review in 2002 " in lieu of review 12 May 1939" saying *"Joyce's Finnegans Wake, parts of which have been published as "Work in Progress", does not admit of review. In 20 years' time, with sufficient study and with the aid of the commentary that will doubtless arise, one might be ready for an attempt to appraise it.*
The work is not written in English, or in any other language, as language is commonly known. I can detect words made up out of

[185]. *The Observer* 7 May 1939.

some eight or nine languages, but this must be only a part of the equipment employed. This polyglot element is only a minor difficulty, for Mr Joyce is using language in a new way.

The easiest way to deal with the book would be to become "clever" and satirical or to write off Mr Joyce's latest volume as the work of a charlatan. But the author is obviously not a charlatan, but an artist of very considerable proportions. I prefer to suspend judgment. If I had had to review Blake's Prophetic Books when they first appeared I would have been forced to a similar decision.

What Mr Joyce is attempting, I imagine, is to employ language as a new medium, breaking down all grammatical usages, all time space values, all ordinary conceptions of context. Compared with this, Ulysses is a first-form primer. In this volume the theme is the language and the language the theme, and a language where every association of sound and free association is exploited. In one of the more lucid passages Mr Joyce appears to be discussing language: "has any usual sort of ornery josser, flat-chested, fortyish, faintly flatulent and given to ratiocination... ever looked sufficiently long at a quite everyday looking stamped addressed envelope?"

What, it may be asked, is the book about? That, I imagine, is a question which Mr Joyce would not admit. This book is nothing apart from its form, and one might as easily describe in words the theme of a Beethoven symphony.

The clearest object in time in the book is the Liffey, Anna Livia, Dublin's legendary stream, and the most continuous character is HC Earwicker, "Here Comes Everybody": the Liffey as the moment in time and space, and everything, everybody, all time as the terms of reference, back to Adam or Humpty Dumpty, but never away from Dublin.

This seems the suggestion of the musical half-sentence with which the work begins: "River run, past Eve and Adam's, from swerve of shore to bend of bay, brings us by a commodious vicus of recirculation back to Howth Castle and Environs."

Who, it may be asked, was Finnegan? Again, I should have been unable to tell, unaided, from Mr Joyce's book. But I gather that

*there is an Irish story of a contractor who fell and was stretched
out for dead. When his friends toasted him he rose at the word
"whiskey" and drank with them. In a book where all is
considered, this legend, too, has its relevance.*

*One concluding note. Mr Joyce in a parody of Jung and Freud
("Tung-Toyd") mentioned "Schizo-phrenia". One might imagine
that Mr Joyce had used his great powers deliberately to show
the language of a schizophrenic mind. He alone could explain
his book and, I suppose, he alone review it".*

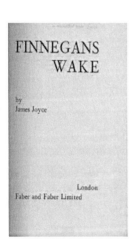

In his book on Samuel Beckett, Anthony Cronin writes of this period,
*Joyce himself suffered a sort of breakdown, drinking and spending
wildly and becoming, like his son, more and more dependent on*

Beckett. Cronin recounts how in a conversation with Joyce on 'this war', James was inclined to see it as an unwarrantable and unnecessary complication of people's affairs and in part a plot to prevent his book from getting the attention it needed [186].

The brothers had drifted apart, though Stanislaus took on the role of rectifying mistaken criticism of James, after his death. Stanislaus died on 16 June 1955.

When the *Irish Times* announced the publication of *Finnegan's Wake* by Sean O'Casey, the Editor RM Smylie visited James to apologise. O'Casey wrote to Joyce, "*I don't think the reference was a misprint. I know many of Dublin's literary clique dislike me, and they hate you; (why, God only knows) so that misprint was a bit of a joke. It is an amazing book, high over my head. I've had constant contact with you in Dubliners, in Portrait and in Ulysses. – that great amazing work".*

---

[186] . Cronin Anthony, *Samuel Beckett The Last Moderninst,Flamingo 1997 p. 3i2.*

CHAPTER 15

DEATH IN ZURICH

Joyce was urged to leave France after the German invasion because as the holder of a British passport he would be interned for the duration of the War. He first left Paris for the Auvergne Region and then sought a return to Zurich. After much support from friendly contacts he received permission to enter Switzerland, arriving in Zurich on 17 December 1940. He had been met at Geneva by the Irish diplomat Sean Lester who was Secretary-General at the League of Nations there. Lester asked Joyce, *"Why do you not go home? I myself would like so much to do so?"* Joyce replied, *"I am attached to it daily and nightly like an umbilical cord"*. He told Lester that it would be undignified of him to return to neutral Ireland during World War II after he had spent almost 40 years in exile and while his only daughter was in a sanatorium in occupied Fence. The family joined in agreeing with Lester's suggestion saying that '*he kept Radio Eireann going on the wireless all the time*'[187]. Lester records that *"Joyce's practical blindness was most noticeable over the tea...I noticed that his wife acted as his eyes"*.

Joyce celebrated Xmas 1940 with friends and a birthday party for his friend Paul Ruggerio on 9 January. He later suffered great pain and was hospitalised. A duodenal ulcer was operated on and he died at 2.15 am on Monday 13 January 1941 aged 58. When Sean Lester heard of the death he was actually posting him an update on Lucia's exit visa prospects. Lester wrote in his diary of 13 January," A great shock...had just written a letter to him about his daughter's case...I

---

[187] . O'Connor Ulick, *The Joyce We Knew* p. 119

am sending a wreath". Joyce had sought the intervention of the Irish government and the international Red Cross to challenge the German authorities' visa refusal for Lucia Joyce. Lester was unable to attend the funeral and suggested to Frank Cremin, *Charge* at Zurich that he might like to go, so that some official Irish person would be there[188]. In the event no Irish official attended.

Harriet Weaver wired money to Nora to help with the funeral costs. Paul Ruggerio sought to persuade Nora to have a priest say the final blessing but she declined. Lord Derwent h the British Minister in Berne was the first speaker at the graveside. He said; *George Moore is gone; Yeats is gone; and now Joyce. But of one thing I am sure – whatever be the rights and wrongs of the relations between England and Ireland, I know Ireland will continue to take the finest and most ironical revenge on us; she will go on giving us great men of letters.* There were several other speakers before the Swiss tenor Max Meili sang the aria '*Tu se' morta* from Monteverdi's opera *Orfeo*. Many efforts were made by friends of Joyce in New York to have a Mass said for him there. *But every priest approached, even the Jesuits whose pupil he was and for whom he preserved great respect, refused on the grounds of Joyce's alienation from the Church. I will always remember that Father George Ford, the Catholic chaplain of Columbia, had the ordinary prayers said for Joyce in Corpus Christi Church[189].*

Under a copy of a painting of Joyce done in Paris by the later Patrick Touhy RHA, the *Irish Press* reported on 14 September 1941: *"James Joyce the Irish writer whose work provoked widespread discussion, died in a Zurich hospital yesterday. Born in Dublin in 1882, he was the son of a Parnellite organiser. He was educated at Clongowes, Belvedere, and University College.*
He later went to Paris where he studied medicine and music. Joyce

[188]. ibid pp. 123-4.
[189]. Colum Mary & Padraig p. 207.

*was a man of extraordinary energy. He never dictated his work, but
wrote it labourisly, re-writing several times if necessary.*

*For many years he fought against failing sight, using a big red pencil,
and writing letters so large that a few words filled each page.   He
usually worked 14 hours a day without rest. As a student he showed
talent of a rare order. His first publication was an essay entitled
"The Day of the Rabblement" which was printed with Francis
Sheehy-Skeffington's "A Forgotten Aspect of the University
Question" in a twopenny pamphlet now very rare, on October 15
1901.*

*In 1907 he published "Chamber Music" a volume of lyrics. His other
works before going to live on the Continent included "Dubliners " a
collection of stories abut the Capital's personalities and in 1914 "The
Portrait of the Artist as a young Man", a semi autobiographical work.
He left Dublin about 1916 and spent the remainder of his life on the
Continent, living at various times in Rome, Trieste, Paris and Zurich.
Ulysses which took many years to write was published in 1924 in
Paris. Its circulation was banned in many countries on moral
grounds. It provoked bitter controversy beimg furiously attacked by
many critics and praised as a masterpiece by others. Work in Progress
another publication with a Dublin background appeared
intermittently between 1927 and 1932.*

*In some of his work Joyce used the English language in such unusual
forms and without punctuation, that its meaning is not always clear. It
is agreed however that earlier books, such as "Dubliners" and
"Portrait of the Artist as a Young Man" have a permanent place in
great literature. Mr Joyce married Nora Barnacle daughter of
Thomas Barnacle of Galway in 1904. They had one son and one
daughter.*

Constantine Curran wrote in the *Irish Times of 14 January*, *"His later
life belongs to world literature, where his influence has been as
widespread, and profound and as disruptive as that of Picasso in*

painting. He was as great a master of English prose as Yeats was of English verse'. Kenneth Reddin wrote in the same paper, 'Joyce was worth a dozen Irish legations in any country he had chosen to live in. All European writers knew of him, and he took care to let them know that he was Irish. In making Dublin famous he made Ireland famous in European letters'.

The grave was numbered 1449 and 'was meant to be temporary, until Nora could get him repatriated to Ireland, and she asked Harriet to look into this. Harriet approached Count O'Kelly, the Irish charge d'affaires in Paris, but the hostility to Joyce among the Catholic clergy, scholars and politicians was so intense that the request was refused. Nora never forgave this refusal...'[190].

Elizabeth Bowen supported a repatriation writing in the *Bell* of March 1941, 'Let us strip from Joyce the exaggerations of foolish intellectual worship he got abroad, and the notoriety he got at home, and take him back to ourselves as a writer out of the Irish people, who received much from our tradition and was to hand on more'.

The Colums received a last letter from Nora Joyce Zurich in 1951. It read

I really don't know how to thank you and your friends for your very kind gesture in sending me two remittances of 50 and 40 dollars. You can't imagine what a help it is for me to receive some financial aid as I have not received any money from England for seven months except £20. Luckily my solicitor was able to arrange that I get some of the royalties direct from America. It is very difficult for me because I have to support Georgio who has absolutely not a penny of his own and can't get work here. I am so glad that you saw Stephen [the Joyce's grandson] and fid him such a fine boy. Georgio did all he could for him while he was here.

I am afraid I shall sooner or later have to sell my manuscript of

[190]. Bowker, Gordon, *James Joyce A Biography*, Phoenix 2012, p. 534.

'Chamber Music' written in Dublin in the year 1909 and dedicated to me; it is written on parchment and bound in cream coloured leather with the Joyce crest on one side of the cover and our initials on the other side. If you know anybody who you think will be interested in buying such a work would you kindly let me know.

Please convey my best thanks also to Mr Sweeney and Mr. Healy for the very welcome financial help.

With warmest thanks to you and Molly and with kind regards,

Sincerely yours,

Nora Joyce[191].

After the repatriation of the body of WB Yeats to Ireland from France in 1948 there was further speculation that the same might happen with Joyce. Nora was in favour as the family grave already existed in Glasnevin Cemetery in Dublin. This did not happen as the Irish Government, through Sean MacBride, refused to implement such a move[192]. Nora was very disappointed. Sean MacBride, the son of Maud Gonne and Major John MacBride, was then Minister of ExternalAffairs in the Irish Government.

Harriet Weaver became the executor of Joyce's will and set about collecting his manuscripts still available to the family. The main one was that of *Finnegan's Wake* which she intended to donate to the National Library of Ireland. Nora did not approve as she was annoyed that her husband's body had not been repatriated to Ireland. This despite later receiving a letter from Sean MacBride to tell her that the Irish Government was proud to claim James Joyce as *"one of the greatest Europeans of all time"* and also a son of Ireland. Nora decided that instead the British Museum should be the recipient. Harriet Weaver wrote to the Director of the National Library of Ireland, Dr. RJ Hayes, *"I did not discuss with Mrs Joyce the disposal of the manuscript of A Portrait of the Artist as a Young Man which*

[191] . Mary and Padraig Colum, Our Friend James Joyce, gollancz 1959. P. 238-9.
[192] . Mulhall Ed   Irish Times. Century Ireland 1913-1923.

Mr. Joyce gave me a long time ago. I should like to give this to the National Library of Ireland if you would care to have it. It is really a fair copy made for the typist and without corrections. I should also be pleased to give you for the library – and I think Lucia Joyce would be pleased too – the wonderful illuminated initial letters she made (urged on by her father) for the Chaucer A.B. C."

Miss Weaver presented the manuscript of *Portrait* of *the Artist* to the Irish Ambassador in London, FH Boland for transmission to the National Library in Dublin[193].

Nora died on 10 April 1951 after receiving the last rites of the Catholic Church. Initially, due to a lack of space, she was buried apart from her husband but they now share the same grave, together with their son Georgio and his second wife in Fluntern Cemetery Zurich.

Lucia Joyce spent the last thirty years of her life in St Andrew's Hospital in Northampton England. She received visits from Samuel Beckett, Sylvia Beach, Frank Budgen, Maria Jolas and Harriet Weaver and Samuel Beckett helped with the cost of her care. Nora Joyce did not have a good relationship with Lucia and never visited her at any of the institutions she attended. Lucia died in 1982 and is buried in Kingsthorpe Cemetery in Northampton.

---

[193] . Platt Len, *James Joyce Texts and Contexts*, Continuum London & New York 2011. Note 488.

The Joyce family grave Glasnevin Cemetery Dublin.

Lucia's Grave 1907-1982.

Joyce's grave in Fluntern cemetery Zurich

Chapter 16.

THE JOYCE TOWER & MUSEUM AT SANDYCOVE

During the September of 1904, James had once again faced
accommodation problems in Dublin. He did not like staying with the
Cousin's at Dromard Terrace in Sandymount. They were too *'good'*.
His Aunt Josephine Murray took him in but his late hours annoyed
her husband and he was locked out. He then went to live briefly at the
Martello Tower[194] at Sandycove, with his antagonist Oliver St. John
Gogarty, who had rented it from the Secretary for War at eight pounds
for the year. Gogarty writes that Joyce *"as good as his word stumped
up the rent from a prize that he had won in some examination"*. Joyce
also left a roll of manuscripts in the Tower before they moved in as an
article of possession. These Towers are of very sturdy construction,
with solid stone walls eight feet thick, having a staircase built in the
thickness of the walls. They are comprised of two floors with a gun
platform on top for two or three guns, and also a place for pouring
molten lead or burning oil down on the unfortunate enemy who
approached it. In a covered recess on the roof is a place for heating
cannon balls…the towers can only be entered by mounting an iron
ladder leading to a door twenty feet above the ground. The door could
only be opened by a copper key which would not give off sparks[195].

Martello towers, so called, from Cape Mortella in Corsica, were built by the British in 1804 as a defence against
a threatened Napoleonic invasion. The one at Sandycove is open to the public throughout the year and
contains a wide variety of artefacts linked to Joyce. It flies a 'Munster' flag referred to in the Cyclops section of
Ulysses, "the flag of the province of Desmond and Thomond, three crowns on a blue field, the three sons of
Milesius". Ulysses, Wordwell, p. 296.
[195] . *The Blarney Magazine* 1955.

They had been built in anticipation of an invasion by Napoleon Bonaparte, which never happened. The Tower at Sandycove had many visitors who stayed with Gogarty, including Arthur Griffith and Seumas O'Sullivan.

The relationship between Gogarty and Joyce was a love-hate one. Gogarty was three years older than Joyce. They were both poets and scholars engaged in *'an apostate of irreverence'* and were inseparable for a year.[196]. James saw Gogarty in the Tower as a Renaissance prelate. Gogarty saw himself as a Roman, a man of the camp and the senate, speaking a language of order and command[197].

In early September an Englishman named Samuel Chenevix Trench who was a keen student of all things Irish, was also staying in the Tower. One night around one thirty Trench awoke from a nightmare screaming *"Ah, the black panther!"* He then fired a gun at the panther and fell back asleep. Gogarty took the gun. Trench awoke again screaming and Gogarty fired some shots over where Joyce lay. He became panic-stricken and scrambled out, dressed, took his ash plant, and left the Tower with Gogarty who was going to swim in the Forty Foot[198]. This forms the opening scene of *Ulysses*, where Trench is known as Haines[199]. I find it interesting that Joyce does not use the name Forty Foot, given his predilection for names. He writes of Buck Mulligan Stephen Dedalus and Haines going down to the Forty Foot;

they followed the winding path down to the creek. Buck Mulligan stood on a stone, in shirtsleeves, his unclipped tie rippling over his shoulder. A young man clinging to a spur of rock near him moved slowly frogwise his green legs in the deep jelly of the water...Buck

---

[196]. O'Connor Ulick, *Oliver St John Gogarty*, Johnathan Cape 1964, p. 64.

[197]. *Colum Mary*, p. 69.

[198]. The Forty Foot is the name of a bathing place amid the rocks near the Tower. The origin of the name is unclear. One theory says that a 40th Regiment of the British army was based nearby at Monkstown and the soldiers were regularly marched to the spot to bathe. An ordinance Survey Map of 1841 contains the name. Visitors to the Tower often ask how it got its name.

[199] .Gogarty Oliver, *It isn't This time of Years at All* pp.68-9.+ pp. 76-7

Mulligan sat down to unlace his boots…He struggled out of his shirt and flung it behind him to where his clothes lay.

–Are you not coming in? Buck Mulligan asked

- Later on, Haines said. Not on my breakfast

Stephen turned away. –I'm going Mulligan, he said.

-Give us that key, Kinch, Buck Mulligan said, to keep my chemise flat.

Stephen handed him the key. Buck Mulligan laid it across his heaped clothes.

And twopence, he said, for a pint. Throw it there.

Stephen threw two pennies on the soft heap. Dressing, undressing. Buck Mulligan erect, with joined hands before him, said solemnly:

-He who stealeth from the poor lendth to the Lord. Thus spoke Zarathustra.

His plump body plunged.

- *We'll see you again, Haines said, turning as Stephen walked up the path and smiling at wild Irish.*
- *Horn of a bull, hoof of a horse, smile of a Saxon. The ship, Buck Mulligan cried. Half twelve.*
- *- Good, Stephen said.*
- *He walked along the upwardingcurving path.*
- *Lilata rutilantium*
- *Turma circumdet*
- *Iubilantium te virginum.*
-
- *The priest's grey nimbus in a niche where he dressed discreetly. I will not sleep here tonight. Home also I cannot go.*

- *A voice, sweettoned and sustained, called to him from the sea. Turning the curve he waved his hand. It called again. A sleek brown head, a seal's, far out on the water, round.*
- *Usurper.*

Michael Scott the architect and Joycean enthusiast, purchased the Martello Tower in 1954, with help from John Huston. In 1978 an exhibition hall was added and a new entrance installed at ground level. Over the years the museum collection has greatly expanded, thanks to the generosity of many donors, which include Paul Ruggiero and Samuel Beckett.

On June 16 1962, the Martello Tower was officially opened as a museum by Sylvia Beach, the American lady who had first published *Ulysses* under the imprint of her Parisian bookshop, *Shakespeare and Company* in 1922. Miss Beach's relationship with Joyce had been triumphant, bittersweet, sacrificial and commemorative. She had become estranged from Joyce over his sale of the rights of *Ulysses* to Random House. She coined the phrase '*Bloomsday*'. She commented that Joyce "*felt that he was persecuted in Dublin though I think that he did as much persecuting as being persecuted*".

The *Observer* of 17 June 1962 reported:

Miss Sylvia Beach performed the opening ceremony. She hoisted the Milesian flag of three Crowns on a blue field mentioned in the Barney Kiernan episode of Ulysses. Among those present were writers, artists, friends and relations of Joyce. [including his two sisters, Mrs Shaurek and Mrs Monagham] and groups from Paris and the USA. Miss Beach said of Joyce, "I met him at a party of the French poet Andre Spire...I should say he was shy. He was very sensitive... Joyce had no small talk. He listened more than he talked... He could recall anything from years back....Joyce was very fond of family portraits and had them up in his house. He had an ancestor cult.

Miss Beach's hosts in Dublin had been Niall and Monica Sheridan. Miss Beach wrote to Monica on 25 June from the Kensington Palace Hotel in London, *I can't tell you how much your kindness and Niall's touched me and how happy I was at your house...It was terribly sad to say goodbye to you and I shall miss you and long to see Ireland again. As we flew over to this country I couldn't bear losing sight of yours and was quite melancholic and homesick. Saw the Tower for a minute as we left Dublin. Aer Lingus was perfect.*

On 7 July she wrote to Niall from her home in Savoie,

the honour of being in your company beside the James Joyce Tower. I hope the Joyceans in America will interest themselves in the Tower's financial future and contribute any Joyce items available for the Museum. We must prod them. I found an ivy brooch of Joyce's old jeweller's and will give it to Margaret to take to you when she comes to Paris...

Miss Beach wrote again to Niall on 6 September saying,

Thinking of you and Monica and remembering your many kindnesses on my unforgettable visit to Dublin. I can't tell you how deeply happy it made me to be welcomed with such warmth! It was as if I were becoming an Irish citizen and I was mighty proud of it[200].

Miss Beach died later that same year of 1962. In December Maria Jolas[201] replied from Paris to a letter from Monica Sheridan commenting on the death of Miss Beach,

Yes, Sylvia's death and the manner of it was a great shame...I believe I am right when I say that the Joyce Tower opening and the gay time she had with you all in Dublin was the crowning event of those last

---

[200] . MS 41,738 NLI

[201] . Maria Jolas and her husband Eugene were among Joyce's closest friends in Paris between the wars. It was she who had suggested that Miss Beach make the trip to Dublin. On Bloomsday 1977 Maria Jolas herself aged 84, visited Dublin for the 6th International Joyce Symposium at Trinity College. After a presentation of music from the works of James Joyce she said, "This *was a wonderful concert, and especially meaningful to me; because the last time I heard many of these songs, Joyce himself sang them*".

years. It was wonderful that it could be so...As for addresses...you don't seem to be aware that Adrienne Monnier[202] took her own life some 5/6 years ago, desperate over her increasingly unbearable rare form of deafness... [Meniere's Disease]

The Martello Tower Sandycove, with new entrance.

[202] . Adrienne Monnier [1892-1955] was a French bookseller, writer and publisher in Paris. Her bookshop was across the road Miss Beach's famous shop.

The 85 year old Sylvia Beach is guided down the steps by Niall
Sheridan at Joyce Tower in 1962. Mary Lavin is behind Miss Beach.
Donal Fallon is the man wearing the glasses.

Joyce's stick, waistcoat, cigar case and guitar at Joyce Tower.

The Irish State recognised James Joyce by the commission of a new ship, named after him in 2015.

Michael Scott.

SELECT   BIBLIOGRAPHY

Barry Kevin, ed. *James Joyce Occasional Writings,* Oxford University Press, 2008

Stewart Bruce, *A Short Literary Life of James Joyce* in,

Bowker, Gordon, *James Joyce A Biography*, Phoenix 2012

Budgen Frank, *James Joyce and the Making of Ulysses*

Byrne JF. The Silent Years*, An Autobiography with Memoirs of James Joyce and Our Ireland,* Farrar, Straus and Young, New York 1935

Clarke Barrett George Moore, *Intimate Portraits* 1951

Colum Mary and Padraig, *Our Friend James Joyce*, Gollancz 1959.

Costello Peter, *James Joyce, The Years of Growth 1882-1915. A Biography, Kyle Cathli Ltd. 1992.*

Ellmann Richard, *James Joyce*, Oxford University Press.1983

Geber Stan *James Joyce* Granada

Gillet Louis*, * Claybook *for James Joyce Ablelard-Schuman 1958*

Gorman Herbert *James Joyce, a Definitive Biography* London 1941.

Groden Michael, *The Complete Simplicity of James Joyce* p. 107 & 116, in *James Joyce* by Sean Latham.

Jordan Anthony J. Jordan, *WB Yeats. Vain, Glorious, Lout; A Maker of Modern Ireland.* Westport Books 2003.

Jordan Anthony J. *Arthur Griffith with James Joyce & WB Yeats – Liberating Ireland* Westport 2013   Joyce

Stanislaus *My Brother's Keeper* ed. Richard Ellmann Faber 1958

Kiberd Declan, *Inventing Ireland* Vintage 1996   Latham

Sean Ed. *James Joyce*, IAP 2010

Lyons FSL, Culture and Anarchy in Ireland 1890-1939. Clarendon Press 1979.

Maddox Breda *Nora A Biography of Nora Joyce*, Hamish Hamilton1988

Mason & Ellmann, Critical Writings of James Joyce 1989.

McCourt John, *The Years of Bloom, James Joyce in Trieste 1904-1920,* the Lilliput Press 2000 .

Norburn Roger, A James Joyce Chronology, Palgrave MacMillan 2004.

O'Brien Edna, *James Joyce*, Weidenfeld & Nicholson 1999

O'Connor Ulick Ed. *The Joyce we Knew* Brandon 2004

O'Higgins Michael D. *When Idea Matter, Head of Zeus UK, 2016.*

Platt Len, *James Joyce Texts and Contexts,* Continuum London & New York 2011

Price Stanley, *James Joyce and Italo Svedo,* Somerville Press 2016.

Read Forrest Ed. Letters of Ezra Pound to James Joyce 1967

Sheehy Richard *May it Please the Court My Lord* p. 27-28.

Sullivan Kevin, *Joyce Among the Jesuits* Columbia University Press 1958.

Tobin Colm, *Penguin Book of Irish Fiction 2001.*

Ungar Andras, *Joyce's Ulysses as National epic* University Press Florida 2002.

Woolfe Virginia, *A Writers Diary.*

INDEX

Finns Hotel 47, 88, 95

Finnegan's Wake 157,171-4

Fitzgerald Desmond 147,157

Fleishmann Marthe 118,157

Fluntern Cemetery 180

Ford Fr. 176

Fortnightly Review 34-36

Forty Foot 184-5

Francini 54, 56, 69, 80

Furey Michael 47, 97

Freemans Journal 24, 32

GAA 73, 152

Gallagher Brendan 22

Galvin Nanny 14

Galway 46, 66,84

Gas from a Burner 100-1

Gasthaus Hoffung 53

Gaelic League 73

Geber Davies Stan 106

Hallstrom Per 158

Harrington Tim 60

Healy Michael 161

Healy Tim 20

Healy Mrs 47

Heaney Marie 17, 157

Hemmingway Ernest 144

Higgins MD 147

Home Rule 123

Hone Joseph 80, 96

Horniman Annie 67

George Lloyd 124

George V 90, 92

Gibbons Luke 6, 146

Gide Andre 7, 169

Gillet Louis 144

Gladstone W 123

Glasnevin 179

Gogarty O. 30, 43-5, 62, 76, 81, 171, 183

Golgotha 28

Gonne Maud 40, 55,111, 152

Gorman Herbert 125

Gordon Bennett Cup Race 42

Gosse Edmund 107, 144

Gregory Lady 6, 35, 40, 66, 145

Grant Richards 56, 59, 76-77, 92

Grave No. 1449, 178

Gresham Hotel 85

Griffith Arthur 5, 31, 37-38, 40-41, 62-65, 72-75 ,98-100, 123, 125, 137-8, 149-3, 159

Groden Michael 96, 146

Horse Show Week 99

Howth 95

Huebsch Ben 110, 133

Hyde Douglas 167

Ibsen 28-9, 34-5, 62

Il Fenianismo 74

Il Piccolo 55, 70, 103

Irish Literary Theatre 33,37

Irish National Epic 99

Irish Parliamentary Party 60, 71, 123

Ivy Day at the Committee 89

Major
JOHN
MacBRIDE
1865-1916
'MacDonagh & MacBride
& Connolly & Pearse'.
Anthony J. Jordan

Price: £8.95

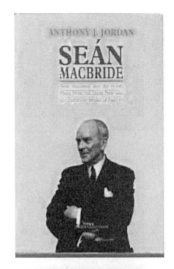

ANTHONY J. JORDAN

SEÁN
MACBRIDE

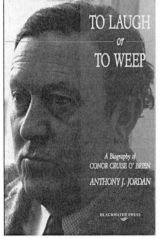

TO LAUGH
or
TO WEEP

A Biography of
CONOR CRUISE O' BRIEN

ANTHONY J. JORDAN

BLACKWATER PRESS

CHURCHILL
a founder of modern
IRELAND

ANTHONY J. JORDAN

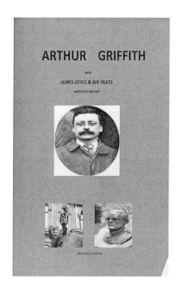

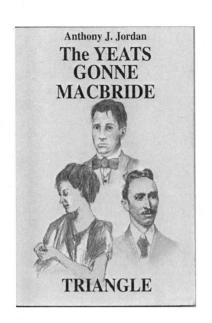

Anthony J. Jordan

The YEATS GONNE MACBRIDE

TRIANGLE

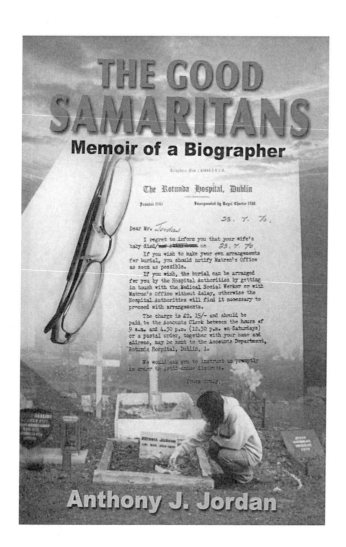

THE GOOD SAMARITANS

Memoir of a Biographer

Anthony J. Jordan